M000015168

# Military Life
# Service or Career

# Military Life
# Service or Career

## A Soldier's Perspective

John McClarren

JMAC Publishing

johnrmcclarren.com

ISBN-13: 978-1500714659
ISBN-10: 1500714658

Cover photo by Charlee Vale.
Book design and graphics by WhiteBoard Design Graphics.
Back cover photo by Deb McClarren.

Additional copies of this book can be purchased from any bookstore or ordered directly from JMAC Publishing: johnrmcclarren.com.

Published by JMAC Publishing
johnrmcclarren.com

Printed by createspace.com

41027090-8

This book is dedicated to all the men and women who have served faithfully in the armed forces of the United States of America; to all who have sacrificed some, and particularly to those who have sacrificed all.

## TABLE OF CONTENTS

COMMENTS FROM THE FIELD .............................................11

INTRODUCTION ................................................................15

CHAPTER 1 – TRAINING ....................................................23

CHAPTER 2 – DEVELOPING SELF-DISCIPLINE.............45

CHAPTER 3 –MATURITY AND RELATIONSHIPS............53

CHAPTER 4 – STRESS: ABSOLUTELY CRITICAL ............69

CHAPTER 5 – TRANSITIONS ...........................................111

CHAPTER 6 – WOMEN IN THE MILITARY ...................147

CHAPTER 7 – OVERSEAS ASSIGNMENTS......................155

CHAPTER 8 – CONFRONTING "OTHER" LIFE ............167

CHAPTER 9 – WILD AND CRAZY THINGS ...................181

CHAPTER 10 – AFTER ALL IS SAID AND DONE .........203

ABOUT THE AUTHOR.......................................................217

ABREVIATIONS.................................................................219

THANK YOU ....................................................................221

DISCLAIMER ...................................................................223

## COMMENTS FROM THE FIELD

I found this book very interesting and well written, and I believe it should be a required read for anyone who might be considering serving their country in the military or making the military a career. It could be a tremendous aid in helping them to decide whether or not the military is right for them.

I found a maturity with this author, seldom found in people whose superiors try to interfere with their retirement. His stories added much to the book. I loved them, and my interest perked up with each one.

As a person who was drafted, served time in the US Army, including almost a year in Vietnam in an infantry reconnaissance platoon, and honorably discharged, I found this book well worth reading. It is filled with very important and interesting details, stories and experiences that will hold a reader's attention, as well as helping him or her with making the right decision regarding a military career, military service or neither.

After serving my country and completing my college education, I worked for 35 years with Workforce

Development, most often referred to as the Unemployment Office. Now called the Career Center in Kentucky, it appears to me that my whole career has been in the area for which this book was written. Military recruiters often used our office to locate individuals to fill their military branch needs. I could identify well with most, if not all, of the content. I now wish this book had been available to me during my career with Workforce Development.

*Ray Lanham (Vietnam 1969-1970)*

MILITARY LIFE: A SOLDIER'S PERSPECTIVE is a must-read book. LTC McClarren shows how making the right career choice and having the determination to breach all obstacles can lead to a life of rewards and success both in the military and in civilian life. He has written a well organized and easy to read book which includes stories that stimulate the emotions and hold your interest.

The author escorts you through his world travels and adventures, and he poses some very thought-provoking questions, which give you a great deal to think about. He relates his stories in ways that will help his readers in their decision-making process, as well as reaching out to those who have had similar experiences and can identify with them. He presents his readers with a great deal of information, both positive and negative, in order to help them determine if the military is right for them, and does it in a way that seems as though he is talking directly to them. By the end of the book the reader will have a firm grasp of what the book title really implies.

Throughout my own life I have developed a fairly extensive process by which to evaluate people. I first met 2nd Lt. McClarren in the Republic of South Vietnam in 1967 when he was reassigned to our company, as my platoon leader from another light infantry brigade further north in the country. Almost immediately, I and the rest of the platoon felt that we could trust him and we all felt very comfortable with him as our new leader. He could talk to us as real people and communicate in a way that many other leaders are not able to. He writes those principles in his book and showed us way back then that he practiced what he believes. He was a well-trained, educated, motivated officer whose confidence transferred over to his men. We had confidence in ourselves as well as him, and it was obvious that his feelings were the same for us.

Lt. McClarren led us through extremely dangerous situations in a combat environment, only too often under intense enemy fire. He motivated us to fight harder, accomplish the mission, and survive the worst of conditions in order to fight another day. He believed in his men, and we trusted him. It was an honor to serve with a "true leader of men" and a real professional soldier.

*Wallace R. Rushing (Vietnam 1967-1968)*

# Introduction

In the pitch-black darkness of an open rice paddy a streak of lightening awakens us from a mesmerized state, followed by a clap of thunder, rattling us to the core. We are then drenched by torrential rain, all of those things expected during the summer monsoons of Southeast Asia. We have set up our night position, complete with razor-sharp concertina wire surrounding our company perimeter, unusual for us, unless trouble is anticipated.

We have been in heavy contact with North Vietnamese Army (NVA) regulars most of the day, and there is no doubt in anyone's mind that our enemy is still nearby tonight. The night rolls on, and the rain is not letting up. We are laying in rice paddies with water up to our shoulders, plagued with that physical stress, and at the same time the mental stress of an anticipated, impending attack. Just as suddenly as the first clap of thunder broke the stillness of the night, automatic weapons fire suddenly interrupts the monotony of the falling rain. Along with those bursts of gunfire are the resounding rocket-propelled grenade (RPG) explosions, as well as those from our own grenade launchers and hand grenades, lighting up the sky and the surrounding area just enough to spot, momentarily, a phenomenal number of NVA regulars charging our perimeter.

Our bodies tingle, our muscles flex and our reflex reactions sharpen to a hair trigger. There are NVA everywhere! Never have we seen so many of them all at one time. We open up with everything we've got, whether or not we can see our targets. Every shot counts, as this is no time to run short on ammunition. The enemy charging us, and the dead hanging in the wire, give an eerie feeling, which increases as they continue to come through the wire.

As this insane fire fight persists, now with our own artillery rounds landing closer and closer, adding to its effectiveness and to the chaos, an RPG round whizzes by my head and sticks in the mud dyke against which I am lying, hardly three feet away from my head! The man closest to me is my platoon sergeant, Sergeant Joe Terrell, and that round is right between us! This is the most terrifying experience probably in either of our lives, not just because this has been a close call; we have already had plenty of those. It is, rather, because it is looking death right in the face, as the two of us are watching that round, waiting for a delayed detonation to end our lives right here and now.

This horrid firefight persists for what seems like an eternity, and then, as suddenly as it began, it is over. The enemy has seen that he is not going to be successful in his attempt to overrun our position, though we can never say that he did not give it his best effort. He, in all of his well-developed stealth, fades off into the darkness, and all is again still.

We gather our thoughts, reorganize our units and begin the evacuation of our dead and wounded, and through the early morning light we can see a good deal of what we had encountered a short time before. Bloody enemy bodies litter the scene of the battle, some still hanging in the wire. We also have our own dead and wounded to care for. That is the only time I have ever seen a man (enemy soldier) hit directly in the head with an M-79 grenade. His brain matter is spread over a wide area, a sight that no one ever needs to see, leaving a sickness in our stomachs and numbness in our minds, but it is over, and most of us have survived the night.

That is war, and that is what we infantry soldiers do. The Marines are always asking for "a few good men" (or women), and the rest of the armed forces need even more than that. Are you up for the challenge? Read on. This book will show you the realities of military life, both in a combat environment, and in the everyday life on the home front and in areas that are not dealing with the toils of combat.

"Hey, if all else fails, you can always fall back on the military." For decades we heard such comments in the midst of serious job searches while seeking that "meaningful" career. That type of attitude has dissipated considerably over the years, yet I am convinced the idea still persists in the eyes of many.

"If all else fails?" What could those who utter such comments be thinking? They seem to lack an understanding that, without a doubt, the military can provide some of the greatest adrenaline rushes, the most phenomenal adventures, and some of the best avenues for personal growth and maturity that exist anywhere. Nothing can compare with the variety of opportunities for developing as an individual with as little as a four-year enlistment or developing a fantastic career in twenty years. The military has some of the greatest benefits and certainly provides one of the best retirements of any American industry. If one were to fail in the military, he or she would have no recourse but to "fall back" on civilian life.

Have you personally ever contemplated the idea of the military as an option for a rewarding career choice? Perhaps you have already had the military experience, and enjoy going back on occasion to reminisce those old experiences and significant events that had an impact upon your life. Maybe you have had strong opinions about war in general, the Korean War, the Vietnam War, or other more recent wars and military conflicts. You might well have wondered about the total military experience, and would like to hear about it from an insider's perspective. Many people who are interested in the military as a way of life may not have considered the difficulties of making transitions from civilian to military life and then back again. All of these considerations and more will show up in the pages to follow, and my intention is to cover the appealing aspects of military life, as well as those less appealing, concentrating more on the former, both in peacetime and wartime situations.

Just as in any other walk of life, the military is different for everyone who has that experience. You may be one who absolutely loves that type of life, or you may well hate every moment of it. You are the only one who can make that determination, and, if you are trying to make a career decision, you are also the only one who can decide if this is the type of life you would enjoy, and at which you would probably succeed. Let's face it, some people are just not cut out for the regimented life of a soldier, marine, airman or sailor. Others are born for it and should not miss such an opportunity. My personal experiences are with the United States Army and, therefore, it may seem that the emphasis is so oriented. If you are not interested in the Army, but rather another branch of the service, stay with me, because most of the ideas apply to any branch of military service. In fact, my own original inclination was not at all toward the Army, but rather the US Air Force. It was only circumstances that dictated where I was to end up, and I have never had regrets about that choice.

In making a decision as to whether or not the military is right for you, there are so many considerations that go into that decision that it is difficult to cover them in a single book. When I think about one of the primary considerations, I am reminded of a movie I once watched, which at the time I did not think was all that good. The film was called "Bad Teacher," and starred Cameron Diaz and Justin Timberlake. I recall a part in the story where Cameron Diaz, who plays the "bad teacher," tells her friend that she chose all the right reasons for becoming a teacher. She mentioned all her summers free, holidays during the year, short work days, teaching a subject that did not require a great deal of thinking (middle or junior high school), and several other things she thought were so important. None of the things she mentioned were even realistic, let alone important to the profession or why people should choose to go into education. She was totally out of the realm of reality, and that was one of the primary things that made her such a bad teacher.

While you are considering the military as an occupation or a profession, if that is what you are doing, you have to ask yourself why you might be interested in that field as an occupation, whether it is for four years or thirty years. You have to have a strong desire to serve your country. You have to be willing to make great sacrifices and put your life on the line, put the lives of others before your own, and believe in what you are doing. Are you thinking that you want the military because you have always loved war movies and love the idea of firing up the bad guys? If that is the case, then you are as delusional as Cameron Diaz was about the teaching profession. You would be going into a profession with the wrong ideas of what it is all about. You can have all the wonderful things that military has to offer, but it will not be handed to you on a silver platter. There will be a price. You have heard the phrase, "Freedom is not free," and that is the primary focus we have in the military. We fight for the freedoms that we all enjoy in this country, and sometimes those freedoms cost us our lives. Those of us who are professional military people are more than willing to take those chances. Are you?

I'm sure, millions would attest to the fact that the military can be an extremely rewarding career. Depending upon circumstances in the world, the military life can vary tremendously. As you can well imagine, the military establishment is an entirely different organization when there is a war going on than when peace reigns. The objectives that our country establishes are much different during wartime than during peacetime. The emphasis of training, the attitudes and the general life styles are all very much different as times and the environment change. It helps a great deal to be flexible in order to accept those changes.

Do you sometimes wish that you could have an occupation in which you could serve your country in some way and yet one that could be exciting, adventurous, even intellectually challenging? Ideally, it might be one that would never allow you to become bored with the monotony of the same old routine, day after day. The military service could certainly be one option that might fulfill that wish. I will show you the ups and the downs, the humor, the terror, the suspense, the adventure and the personal growth that all can experience with such a life.

I relate all those elements through my own point of view, and the views of many others with whom I've had contact. I'm sure there are many of you who will identify with a number of these experiences. Some may laugh with me, some may thrill with me, and some may even weep with me now and then, but all should be able to enjoy this book and even to learn a bit from it. If you are in the process of planning your life, there may well be some ideas worth pondering within these pages. If you are well along in your current career development, or near or beyond the point of retirement, perhaps you can identify with many of the moments and ideas that I will share, and be moved or even amused by many of the situations and incidents that will follow. It should be a fun read for all. To use the Army Infantry School motto: "Follow me!"

# Chapter 1 – Training

For the armed forces of the United States to maintain superiority throughout the world, a few things are absolutely necessary to maintain a continuing state of readiness. We need to maintain our troop strength, our equipment levels in regard to quality and quantity, and the focus and frequency of training in all branches of the military, and at all levels of command. Indeed, that training can never end, and our country can never weaken its resolve in those efforts, or we will find ourselves diminishing in our effectiveness, only to become a second-rate military force. We cannot afford that. Training for the individual begins the first day the recruit reports for duty. He or she begins basic training, or boot camp, and that is only the beginning phase of a series of training levels through which that man or woman will go. Then, of course, beyond the individual, there is unit training at every level of command, from the squad-, section- or team-sized unit right up to the Commander-in Chief, the President.

Most Americans have heard the horror stories of boot camps from all branches of the military service. There are likely as many versions of the boot camp experience in each branch of the military service as there are people who have experienced it first-hand. Most of the colorful stories that abound probably come from the Marines who have always been notorious for having the toughest of all programs. It is probably still true, but none of these programs is designed to be the proverbial "piece of cake." Most people who have graduated from such training probably perceived it at the time as one of the most difficult experiences of their lives. That feeling, however, generally subsides shortly thereafter and becomes just another invaluable experience that contributes to the overall development of the individual as a Marine, soldier, sailor or airman.

My perspective is that of an old soldier. I was Army most of my life, though I was born and raised in a Navy town, and later thrived among Marines; in this case, "survived" might be a more appropriate term. My experiences with boot camp or basic training were not as traumatic as some might have you believe their experiences were. I started with a distinct advantage, however. I had prior military experience before enlisting in the Army, which included one year of Air Force sponsored Civil Air Patrol in my first year of high school, Army junior ROTC (Reserve Officers Training Corps) in my next two years of high school and a couple of years of Air Force ROTC in college. That put me "miles" ahead of most of my peers, or seemingly so, when in actuality all it did was get me into a good deal more trouble than I would have had without it. The very first thing my drill sergeant did was make me the platoon leader of my basic training platoon.

That certainly brings up an old memory, that of Drill Sergeant Moyer. That man's face is embedded so deeply in my memory banks that I'll take his image to the grave. Some have deeply seated hatred for their old basic training drill sergeants, but that would by no means constitute my feelings for Drill Sergeant Moyer. I have nothing but the utmost respect for that man. I have no clue, of course, whether he is alive or dead today, but, as most of us know, "Old soldiers never die; they just fade away." He has to be one of those. I use this example, because so many who have gone through this experience will be able to identify with it, and my younger readers may well have similar experiences in the future. At the very least, they will be memories forever.

Although it's been nearly fifty years since I've seen the man, I can see his face as clearly as though it had been last week. I remember so vividly how he used to get right in my face, within inches of making contact. He could talk right through anybody's face. For me it was extremely effective, as he and I were the same height and we looked at one another eye to eye. He could not have been more than five feet, six inches tall, and yet he came across as a giant. He had no top teeth to my knowledge; he spoke right through his bottom teeth with his upper lip pressed tightly against them.

As most Army drill sergeants at that time, Drill Sergeant Moyer's language was what most would call colorful. Every other word was an f-word, and yet he had no problem whatsoever with human communication. He could get his point across very clearly to anyone, regardless of that person's intellectual level, and in my training platoon we had every conceivable level. That man could be as mean and nasty as any human could be, and, at the same time, to a select few, as kind, considerate and understanding as anyone could ever imagine. If I had not been placed in a leadership position, I might never have recognized his qualities. I was able to communicate with him in a manner few of the other trainees ever had the opportunity. I was able to see him as a human being, rather than as a basic training drill sergeant, and there was a very big difference between the two. Drill sergeants are expected to be without sentimentality. A warm-hearted drill sergeant would just not fit the stereotype.

Being put in charge of my training platoon had its advantages, but it also had a few significant drawbacks. I managed to avoid such things as KP (kitchen police), guard duty, and other arduous chores, but then again, I was put in charge of the motliest crew you could possibly imagine. That basic training company, and my platoon in particular, consisted of some of the toughest, meanest, ugliest individuals in the world. Well, it sure seemed that way to me.

I entered the Army in October of 1965, a time during which the United States had just started to increase its involvement in Vietnam. Our country was in the process of building up our military, and in that endeavor we also instituted the draft. All branches of service, except the US Coast Guard, were drafting, which did not cease until 1972. As part of that system, those men in trouble with the law were given a form of amnesty, in that they were given a choice: go to jail or be welcomed into the US Army, each as an American fighting man. Well, at least half of those folks must have ended up in my company and in my platoon. There could be some elements of exaggeration there. We did have fine, young men from the streets of Los Angeles, Chicago, Detroit and New York City, to name a few. These "gentlemen" were real thugs, most of them about twice my size, and, again I'm no giant in stature. To be politically correct, I believe I am considered "vertically challenged."

I'm still not sure today how I managed to survive that situation. My job was to make sure these guys were "toeing the line." To do that, I had to be very direct, yet, let's face it, non-offensive. Diplomacy and psychology seemed to be the orders of the day. I had to figure out, with little or no training in such matters, how to make these men get their jobs done, stay out of trouble, and yet not develop a hatred for me. I also wanted them to be the best platoon in the company. In addition, I had the goal of finishing basic training alive, one way or another. Survival became one of my biggest challenges for the next few weeks; actually, a lot longer than that, but we'll get into those stories later.

The whole basic training situation was something of an anomaly in that, while we were trying to stay alive through our training, we were in training to learn to survive in a wartime scenario by learning how to kill effectively. Does that make any sense at all? I didn't think so. The real "kill" training came later, however, in advanced (infantry) combat training. The whole idea of Basic Combat Training (BCT) was not to make real soldiers; that would be later. The idea was to "weed out" the "ash and trash" and make soldiers out of the remainder who had at least some chance of success in the military. Let's face the facts; as previously stated, some people are not predestined for military life. They cannot deal with that type of structure and discipline, let alone take orders. It's just not in their designer genes.

So, why would some be so well suited for military life and others not? Many of you have had first-hand experience, and you will easily figure out where I am going with this one. Think about it. Again, we know that there are those who just are not able to take orders from anyone. We often can identify them way back in elementary school. They were the ones who acted up for teachers and school administrators, and it continued all the way through high school. If they never ended up in jail, it was at least a borderline miracle, because they were just never able to follow the rules or the law. They established their own sets of rules, and they were seemingly unable to live under anyone else's, no matter what. Many ended up in gangs.

I think most of the civilian population understands that the military establishment cannot function without a very specific structure. There is a hierarchy of leadership called a chain of command, similar to a civilian corporate structure. It is the only way our military can ensure that we complete our projects and accomplish our missions, particularly in a combat environment.

Our leaders can never afford the luxury of allowing their subordinates to take whatever time they need to think about whether or not an order should be followed. That is one sure way of losing people on the battlefield. Many, however, have found themselves in tight situations and discovered that they followed orders that were in fact unlawful. The consequence of such an event would be that the person following the order is as guilty of wrongdoing as the person who gave it. Sometimes there is a fine line between the two. Nevertheless, the individual who is unable to follow any order will never find success in the military. It takes a good follower to be a good leader. That is a truth I learned long ago.

What about the person who is terribly sensitive about his or her privacy? How much privacy do you suppose one has in military life, particularly in a training environment with a couple of hundred other troops, or in the confines of a military barracks with fifty or sixty other people? There is no such concept as private bedrooms, private bathrooms or private shower stalls. What I am talking about here is one huge room with about thirty sets of bunk beds, with sixty men (or women) all sleeping in the same room. Added to that, of course, would be one large bathroom (head, latrine, whatever) that all sixty would share. One might hope that all sixty people would have similar habits of hygiene, that none would drink, smoke, do drugs or use excessive profanity, to say nothing of a myriad of nastier habits. The ideal situation simply never happens. We are all different; so, how in the world do we deal with that? We frequently just have to endure. We either accept or reject. If it's the latter, then we have another problem; dissension in the ranks.

There are other obvious differences with which we need to contend. Think not only about the cultural differences, but also the intellectual differences. There will be people in the ranks with IQs in the genius category, particularly during times of a draft. There will also be those whose IQs seem to be lower than their age, though not quite so much in today's military, which requires passing the near equivalent of a college entry exam, called the ASVAB (Armed Services Vocational Aptitude Battery). What can all these people ever hope to have in common, and how would you ever expect them to be able to communicate on a common level? Well, it might surprise you if you have never encountered such a situation. If nothing else, these people are all doing the same things together every day.

They eat the same food, use and clean the same bathroom facilities and living areas, go through the same training, undergo the same pain and suffering with early morning PT, standing in ranks, and being harassed by drill sergeants. It is amazing to think about how much they have in common.

Think about trying to get through each night in the barracks. If you are not accustomed to someone in the same room snoring all night long, can you imagine the "symphony" that goes on with fifty or sixty men sleeping in the same room? If you have not experienced it, you cannot imagine it. It's bad enough when you have one guy in the barracks rattling the walls. Add nine or ten at the same time at about the same volume, and what have you got? Try about six on the Richter scale!

On top of the snoring, to which you might in time become accustomed, think about all the other minor distractions. There is the sleepwalker, the sleep talker, the insomniac who paces up and down the squeaky floor all night, and don't forget the intolerant, ex-gang member who leaps out of his bunk and gives our rather defenseless insomniac a body slam to the floor, perhaps leaving him unconscious. Then there are further distractions, such as the MP's (military police) who come to take the assailant away, and the ambulance that comes to haul the victim to the hospital. By this time the entire barracks is awake for the rest of the night, as half the men have been disrupted so much they will not be able to get to sleep again. Of course, it's probably only an hour or two before the drill sergeant will be storming in to rouse the troops anyway. Granted, all nights will not be that bad, but being prepared is wise.

Many people are extremely sensitive about others yelling at them, for what may seem no particularly good reason, and have their feelings hurt. Then again there is the other extreme, when the person decides to lash back at an authority figure and refuses to allow another person to "get in his or her face." Ultimately, it will end up going very badly for that individual. The one who has his feelings hurt and displays that hurt in an obvious way will be ridiculed severely for being a "cry baby" or a "wimp" and the harassment will continue and worsen. The one who lashes back in defense will undoubtedly end up guilty of insubordination, and in more extreme cases will physically assault his superior and end up in the brig or stockade and ultimately in a trial by court-martial. That, of course, could very well result in separation from the service with a less than honorable discharge. Hey, stuff happens.

Yes, it all sounds a bit grim, but the vast majority of those who begin basic training do manage to complete it relatively unscathed. Today's modern military has actually begun to experiment with a new system to deal with stress. Each time a military person has to deal with an overly stressful situation, he or she merely pulls out a "stress" card and has it punched, and no one under any circumstances is allowed to pressure that person in any way for a set period of time. This whole idea tends to drive an old soldier like me close to insanity. The stress card concept, in my opinion, destroys the whole idea of developing a leader; one who is capable of dealing with any kind of stress under any conditions and not having to have psychological counseling as a result of it. It's nonsense! But then that is only my humble opinion. My humility is killing me. However, if I understand correctly, most units in the Army have now changed their ways of thinking. I hope that they have seen the errors of that philosophy.

There are circumstances under which some of our military people experience normal events in life and are unable to deal with them. They have stresses that are more than they can handle. In those situations, it may well be that the person needs psychological help. I would never be one to deny that privilege. If, however, that person were merely unable or particularly unwilling to deal with the stress put upon him by drill sergeants or other training cadre, I would question whether or not that trainee was fit for military duty. The only way any military person can prepare himself for a leadership position is if he is able to deal with the same stresses that are prevalent in a combat environment. That is a primary goal of all leadership courses.

The actual training that transpires in basic training includes self-defense, individual weapons training and qualification, field sanitation, code of conduct, military justice, drill and ceremonies and, of course, let us never leave out physical training. Remember that the abbreviations BCT in the Army stand for Basic Combat Training, the implication being that each soldier is to be first and foremost a fighting man or woman, and then later he or she will concentrate on a specialty. The idea is that in a combat situation, every individual may be called upon to be an "American fighting man" (or woman), and he or she must be prepared for that eventuality.

BCT, or boot camp in branches other than the Army, is an introductory course to all of the above subjects, but not intended to make experts of anyone in any of the subjects listed. If one were to specialize in infantry later on, and go through infantry AIT (Advanced Individual Training), then that person, after successful completion of the course, would be placed into an infantry MOS (military occupational specialty). In the case of infantry, that person would be considered affectionately a "grunt," both in the Marines and the Army.

The same can be said for any choice the individual soldier, sailor or airman makes in regard to special areas of concentration after his basic training. He may wish to be a cook, a clerk, a driver, a mechanic, a tanker, an artilleryman, a medic, or any of dozens of choices, many of which could quite well prepare him for a future career or occupation after transition to civilian life. Many of these areas are at least briefly touched upon during boot camp in order to give all personnel some working ideas to enable them to make the best decisions for themselves and for their future. That, combined with testing each person must go through before his induction, will help the trainee establish and work toward a specific occupation.

Other segments of training during boot camp would include the history of the specific military service and its effects upon US history. The training includes the traditions of military service and what is expected of the individual while on active duty, both in a wartime scenario and during times of peace. There are certain expectations given to military personnel that appear to be far beyond what is generally expected of anyone in the civilian population. A military person, regardless of what branch he or she is in, is expected to look sharp, conduct himself in a gentlemanly or ladylike manner, be above reproach when it comes to honesty and integrity, and present himself or herself as a servant of the people at all times. The above standards apply to all active duty personnel in all branches of service, as well as all reserve components, including the National Guard.

BCT is usually about eight weeks in length, followed by a graduation ceremony. Those who have successfully completed the training are considered soldiers, sailors, Marines or airmen at that point, prepared for their more advanced specialty training in whatever category they have chosen, or which perhaps in wartime has been chosen for them. After their advanced training, most people are ready for assignment to a permanent unit, beginning their real jobs. However, some may desire to go on to other more specialized schools, such as airborne training, Ranger School, special operations training, officer training programs to attain a commission, warrant officer training or NCO academy (leadership training for enlisted personnel to become a non-commissioned officer). Each branch of service offers additional options for further training and advancement.

After basic training there is an advanced course in a field of specialty, or AIT, in any of the fields mentioned, and many others as well. Each branch of the service has its own full array of specialty training. Although discipline is still important, most of the harassment decreases and there is less pressure. The emphasis is on preparing the individual for his or her specialty area in order to insure that he or she does well on the job after completion of the course.

Along with the advanced training, all trainees are offered the opportunity to earn an expert's badge for that specialty. In the infantry it's called an EIB (Expert Infantry Badge). All through training the prospect of achieving that award is probably the major motivation for each person. At the end of training there is a very tough test administered to all who apply for it, and only the best will pass with a high enough score to attain the expert badge. The military has many awards for outstanding performance, and, unlike civilian life, each person has the opportunity to display those accomplishments on his or her uniform for the rest of the world to see. It is very effective in building self-esteem.

Upon completion of advanced training, each individual is assigned a specific MOS (military occupational specialty) and then sent on to a regular unit, as mentioned, wherein he or she can use their newly acquired skills. There are always additional options, however. You may well not want any further schooling or training and just want to move along with your career or obligation, if that is all that you are looking for. On the other hand, there are many who want to reap all the educational benefits that the service has to offer and tackle any courses for which they may be qualified.

One option that could apply to many individuals of any branch of service is airborne training. It probably goes without saying that the primary focus of airborne training is to teach people how to exit an aircraft with a parachute and survive. It would seem in today's military forces that the concept of airborne deployment of forces is all but null and void. My personal observations over the last fifty years have been that mass airborne drops of troops into a combat zone have all but disappeared. We had only two during the entire Vietnam War and those were not taken entirely seriously by most, even those who participated. The participants were awarded combat jump wings, though none ever came under hostile fire during those jumps.

Nearly the same thing occurred in the infamous Granada invasion. I've spoken to several people who participated in that operation, and most are somewhat embarrassed about even receiving combat infantry badges, let alone combat jump wings. Most are at least somewhat reluctant to discuss the subject of Granada at all. The truth is all of them went into a combat environment, not having any idea what to expect, and they were ready for any challenges that might meet them. Consequently, they did earn what they received. It could have been a very dangerous situation, and they were prepared for any eventuality. They were led to believe that they would be met with significant hostile fire.

Nevertheless, even though we no longer employ airborne units in their traditional roles, those units still exist, and we still have the airborne schools to fill the units. Two of the existing Army airborne units are the 82nd Airborne Division and the 173rd Airborne Brigade. In addition to the airborne units still in existence, there continue to be growing requirements from the special operations units and detachments from all of the services, considering today's anti-terrorist activities throughout the world. The vast majority of the Army's Special Forces are airborne qualified personnel. The same may be said of the Army Rangers. Because of our "special operations," most of which consist of very small units, many of the airborne drops are not from fixed-wing aircraft, but rather from helicopters. Again, we're not referring to massive airborne deployments;

only small numbers of people. Those kinds of deployments also require more specialized training than basic airborne training. That is where Ranger School or other more specialized courses come in. Occasionally free-fall jumps are required, the training of which is not employed in standard airborne training at Fort Benning, Georgia or Fort Bragg, North Carolina.

The next logical step for those who are combat arms oriented and feel challenged by what the Army once called being "all you can be" would be to apply to one of those schools in each service that can accommodate that need. The Army has Ranger units, as well as the more specialized Delta force, the Navy has the Seals, the Marine Corps has its Long Range Reconnaissance (Force Recon), and the Air Force has its Special Tactics units, part of the Special Operations Command. These schools fine-tune their people in combat operations tactics, weapons, survival skills, and leadership, as well as training in more specialized areas of operations.

Undoubtedly none of these courses would be complete today without extensive counter-terrorist training. They are not designed to be what I refer to as "gentlemen's" courses. Simply put, not everyone who participates will successfully complete the courses. Many will drop out for physical, mental or academic reasons, as one has to excel in all of those areas, the toughest perhaps being the physical challenges. Some of my personal experiences will appear later in this book. For now, suffice it to say that these schools provide some of the most extraordinary challenges that most will ever encounter in their lives. We never want to send our American troops into a combat situation for which they are not well prepared in advance. That element alone justifies the seemingly inhumane treatment that students face in those schools. I can attest to that through my experiences with the Army's Ranger School.

The Army Special Forces have been in existence since before Vietnam, and have earned some of the highest honors. They have historically been among the best soldiers that the US Army has produced, due to the intense and technical training they receive. The Special Forces units have been known to get themselves into precarious situations in which they have to apply those skills that they have mastered so well. In other words, they have to be John Waynes or Sylvester Stallones in cases of emergency, not because they choose to, but because there is sometimes no choice. That's what they are paid for. It is by the nature of their missions that they sometimes find themselves in those situations. They are technically teachers by trade, but their jobs entail a great deal more than that.

My intentions would always be to imply that the Special Forces are among the unsung heroes of our nation. They have performed far above and beyond the call of duty many times over. They continuously place themselves in harm's way in the performance of their duty. Because of the support they are giving to the people they are training, and working right alongside them, they also become prime targets of the oppressors of those people they are training. Those oppressors can be terrorist groups, drug cartels or anyone who is the enemy of those we are supporting. That is just another reason why they have to be as effective as they have always proven themselves.

Each person develops a specialty for which he is qualified to teach others. These specialties include individual and crew-served weapons, demolitions, communications, first aid, field sanitation, operations and tactics, among others. Most in those units are also foreign language specialists. The ultimate goal is primarily to help third-world armies be more effective in local combat and field operations.

Another special operations training provided by the Army is pathfinder school. Again, this school is considered one of the more elite schools for those who wish to take their training to yet another level. Pathfinders are the people who are trained to go deep into enemy territory and set the stage for offensive operations. If there is to be an airborne phase of the operation, where men and equipment are dropped into a hostile area, the pathfinders are the people who will establish the drop zone and mark it. If there is to be an airmobile operation, with the use of helicopters, then the pathfinders will have established and marked the landing zone for the operation. They need to know how to establish and prepare these areas in the middle of enemy territory, avoiding enemy contact if possible, and how they plan to get themselves out of the area as soon as their mission is accomplished.

As I mentioned, special operations are now a major part of all branches of the military. All of the people who train for these special operations units go through much of the same training, and, in fact, cross train from one service to another. Many of the courses that the Navy, Marines, and Air Force require of their special operations people are only provided by the Army. Some examples which most of them need are airborne training, free-fall parachute training, and Special Forces Combat Divers Training, not to imply that the Navy Seals would send their people to that training. All branches of service provide similar training for their special ops personnel, but, of course, each branch has its own more specialized environments and different sets of criteria requiring a variety of specialties. Each trains for its specific mission. That is a good, concise tactical picture of what today's military represents.

Most of the other schooling in the military establishment is designed for building an advanced knowledge base and developing leadership skills in the individual, for the enlisted, as well as for commissioned officers. There are fundamental leadership schools for enlisted personnel, followed by the NCO Academy, all of which are designed to prepare and qualify those who wish to become non-commissioned officers. There are several sources for commissioning officers at many colleges and universities throughout the country. These include the military academies (Army, Navy, Air Force and Coast Guard Academies), Virginia Military Institute (VMI) and the ROTC programs at most major universities, and a few others not mentioned. For furthering an officer's career, there is an advanced officer course for each branch of service, primarily for Army and Marine captains and Navy lieutenants who intend to be promoted. That is followed by Command and General Staff College for Army and Marine majors and Navy lieutenant commanders who look toward additional promotions, and finally the war colleges for each of the services for senior-grade officers who are selected. In some ways it is like being in the field of education. Each person is expected to continue his or her education if he or she expects to be promoted and to continue with their chosen career or just to retain that job. That is a given.

# CHAPTER 2 – DEVELOPING SELF-DISCIPLINE

Y ou have read a few of the good and bad experiences I have encountered within the military, and, of course, there will be more to follow. I happen to be an old Clint Eastwood fan, and I can never help thinking of the ugly to go along with the good and bad. I also never seem to separate the three into different categories, in that they all seem to blend together as ideas develop. I will show you more examples of what I mean as we progress.

With regard to the first category (good), let's consider some questions: What genuine good can emerge for the improvement of life in general? Can there be a life in the military superior to that in the civilian sector? What are the real differences between civilian life and that of the military? There are many points at which to begin, but let's just start with the most elementary and even the simplest and most obvious; self-discipline.

Self-discipline is so all-important that, without it, survival in the military is not possible. I cannot imagine making it through some of the phenomenal experiences I have had in the military without possessing and/or having developed some degree of self-discipline. Many who end their military careers with less than honorable discharges can probably attribute that end result to a complete lack of self-discipline in their lives. They perhaps had not developed such a quality before entering the military, and more than likely never got the full picture of what the military was trying to accomplish with them. Some are just stubborn, and perhaps had been what we refer to at an earlier age as incorrigible. There is little help for those types if they are not willing to accept the levels of discipline it takes to deal with life in general, let alone military life. If you are in that category, then it is very possible that the military is not the best choice for you.

I would like to relate a single incident of mine from the US Army's Ranger School. That situation occurred sometime in my first three weeks of the Ranger course at Fort Benning, Georgia around March of 1969. The morning ritual was to arise at 0330 hours (3:30 A.M.) and fall out immediately for our three- to four-mile run. Upon completion of the run, we would do our morning calisthenics, a formidable workout for anyone. After that we would do the obstacle course, go back to the barracks, clean up and then go to breakfast. Then the academic part of the day would begin, preceded by our march, or jog, to the training area for the day.

On one of those training days, per usual, we began the obstacle course with a back-crawl under a barbed wire cover for approximately twenty-five meters, through about six or eight inches of mud (good old Georgia red clay). Being nice and gooey and red from that minor obstacle, we went to the parallel ladder, which had always been the proverbial "piece of cake" for me, as my upper body strength was my strongest asset. Beneath the parallel ladder was about three feet of water in trenches dug under each lane. If one were to fall, he'd have a nice soft, though wet, landing, or perhaps submersion is a better term.

The procedure here was to place your left foot on the "step" to allow you to grasp the horizontal bar with both hands, particularly important for people like myself, being "vertically challenged." Upon hearing the command, "Hang free!" you are to drop your legs down, with both feet hanging in the air and both hands grasping the first rung of the ladder, ready to begin your hand-over-hand trip across thirteen rungs to the end. Honestly, for me that was pathetically simple. Unfortunately, for me that day, I did not hear the command, "Hang free!" I did, however, hear my lane-grader/drill sergeant scream out, "You, cheater! I said, Hang free!" I did hang free at that point. After a quick eleven or twelve rungs I heard, "You! Cheater! Turn around and go back!" I did so, and at that point I was not even beginning to breathe any harder than normal.

Well, he did not stop there. Each time I approached the end of the circuit, he would repeat, "You! Cheater! Turn around and go back!" As much upper body strength as I might have had, I was tiring physically faster than my lane grader was tiring of repeating himself. As time went on, and lap after lap ensued, my hands still wet and muddy from the previous obstacle, I began to weaken considerably, yet I knew that I could still keep it up for a few more laps. Finally, my lane grader decided that I would not have the satisfaction of making it to the end of the next lap. He stopped me in the middle of that lap with the command, "Freeze, cheater!" He then shouted, "Drop, cheater!"

Mentally shaking my head and rolling my eyes back, as I would not have wanted the lane grader to have noticed that, I released my grip, dropping a few feet, submerging into the blackness of the murky water below. The predawn hour, of course, made it seem even darker. Attempting to sink my feet into some firm ground, and finding nothing but slimy mud, I managed to rise up out of the water, heading toward the end of the pit, in order to climb out. There was a rubber mat at the end of each lane to assist the ranger trainee in extracting himself from the water-filled pit. If one were to have all of his strength and be reasonably tall, that task would be relatively simple. However, I did not fit either of those categories. I jumped with all of the strength I could muster, and my hands reached very close to the end of the rubber mat, but not quite. The mat was, of course, wet and muddy, as were my hands. My body simply slid, much like an eel, right back into the water. Time and time again I tried, but to no avail. I was not exactly gaining strength with each attempt.

Finally, after what must have been ten tries, I felt my fingers grasp the end of the mat, which gave me a chance to pull myself free of that obstacle. The "cheater" was then forced to low-crawl to each of the next two obstacles, the next being the log obstacle, which rose to a height of probably twenty-five feet, the object of which was to climb up one side and down the other! By the time I reached the last obstacle, a rope climb over another water obstacle, I was sapped of most of my strength. It was all but gone. I was determined, however, that this was not going to defeat me. At least I did not have to wait for anyone; I was, by this time, the last one on the course, as everyone else was off to the showers.

From the edge of that pool of water, bordered by about fifteen feet on all four sides and the water being about four feet deep, I stared at the twenty-five foot rope, suspended straight down to the exact middle of the pool. I was concentrating on what my next move was to be. I had only to leap straight forward less than eight feet, and catch the rope in my hands in order to shimmy up the rope. Visualize this. Giving that rope the utmost of my attention, I leaped through the air, body horizontal to the water, toward the rope. At just the calculated place and moment in time my hands whisked by one another over what should have been the rope. My hands passed, crisscrossing my lower arms, seizing nothing but thin air! It was as though I were momentarily suspended in the air, just long enough to say, "Oh, shit!" Then down I went into the water once again.

As I said, my strength was drained and I had then to pull my body up out of the water at least three feet to where a knot was tied at the bottom of the suspended rope. The object was to pull my body up high enough to grab the knot with my feet in order to use my legs, which still had some strength, for the climb. I used all the strength I had left in my upper-body to pull myself from the water. Finally, I felt the knot with my feet and used my legs to pull myself up to one rather short body length above the knot. That left only a mere twenty feet or so to climb! How easy was that? No problem!

With the rope between my legs, up I went, slowly but surely, one hand over the other, probably six to eight inches at a time; a slow snail's pace at best. It seemed to take hours to make that climb. At the top of the rope was a second rope, leading diagonally down to the edge of the pool below. I merely needed to climb high enough to grab that second rope and slide down to the bottom. Up I continued, closer and closer. I was nearly there, not more than a foot and a half from ultimate victory!

I pulled once again with all of my remaining strength (precious little by that time), and – nothing! My body would go no further. I tried and tried as my arms began to tremble. They just shook, like I was going into some kind of seizure, and would no longer move my body upward. I also felt the pain, the anguish, the frustration and the final defeat of this challenge. At that moment I gave a final, last minute surge of strength, yet it was still not enough.

With an inward release of my frustrations and an outward shriek of "Ahh!" I flared my arms, spread-eagle, released the rope, and plunged nearly twenty-five feet downward into five feet of water. Ugh, in the water again! Even though I gave it a mighty effort, failure prevailed that time. The good news was that my obstacle course was over for the day. Somehow I managed to get out of the water and I was off to the showers to begin my "routine" day. Self-discipline ruled that day, as, rather than letting an adverse situation get the best of me, I just moved right along to the next adventure, whatever it might be, and, by that time, I was ready for anything.

# CHAPTER 3 — MATURITY AND RELATIONSHIPS

As previously shown, many of the good and bad elements of military life can certainly overlap, to the degree that they can no longer be distinguished from one another. An amazing amount of personal growth is likely to emerge from any horrible experience you might undergo. The element of maturity ties into that concept. Military service can be one of the greatest sources in the world for the growth of one's maturity. There are few occupations or lifestyles that can compare.

With regard to experiences that might be lifetime memories and huge contributors to the building of maturity, consider some of the following questions I pose here. Where in the civilian world will one find an opportunity to drive a fifty-ton vehicle fifty or sixty miles per hour off road? I refer, of course, to a tank. I mean, really; be honest. Can you imagine that ever happening in your life, presuming that you are not already, or have been, in the military? How about firing an artillery piece or a machine gun, or throwing a hand grenade? In the police or protective services those sorts of activities might be found, but that is about it.

Have you ever imagined yourself flying a fighter jet either from the ground or off an aircraft carrier? Hey, Bruce Willis might be able to do it from a Hollywood set, with a lot of great stunts, but let's get real here. How about "driving" an entire aircraft carrier? Somebody has to do it. Can you imagine yourself progressing from being the lowest ranking individual in the whole Army or any other service to commanding tens of thousands of people in a period of less than twenty years? Many have achieved it. Certainly not all achieve that much, but the sky is the limit in the military establishment. If accepting that kind of responsibility does not develop maturity, nothing will.

Aside from the experiences you will have and the responsibilities you may accept, there are many other things going on that will contribute to your growth as an individual; more than I could ever list in one book. Listing a few will take a while, and I'll elaborate on them as we progress. Some of the more important things that will affect you and your career while you are in the military are the relationships you establish with other people, organizational skills you will develop, dealing with stresses virtually unknown in civilian life, your ability to make effective and timely decisions, problem solving and survival skills, and, lastly, but certainly not least in importance, building humility within yourself, knowing that you are among America's finest, and, yet, possessing a humble nature. All of these will ultimately lead to the highest possible levels of maturity.

A great deal can be said about the relationships each person will develop within the military. Think about it. You are immediately placed in a group of men or women, sometimes even both sexes together, and you live with those people day and night, twenty-four-seven. You eat with them, sleep with them, train with them, march with them, play and joke with them on and off duty, and go out and party with them during off-duty hours. How can you avoid building lasting relationships with those people?

If we happen to find ourselves (and, yes, I include myself with you, in that I have been there and done it) in a combat environment, as is often the case today, it is a completely different set of conditions. We may still have some of those same old buddies that we had with us all through our training, and we will have made many new friends and other acquaintances. We will still be in some of the same types of environments and under many similar conditions that we experienced in our previous training environments, but this time we have some added conditions that were not present before.

Indeed, when it comes to combat, we find ourselves in hostile areas where there are bad guys out there doing their very best to kill us, many of them literally dying to accomplish that goal. We are all there to protect one another, and life takes on a whole new meaning. We may well never have thought of ourselves as ever intentionally trying to be heroes, but we just automatically do things for others that put us in a dangerous position, and we don't even think about it or hesitate to do what we have to do to ensure the safety of our friends and fellow soldiers. It is difficult to explain how these feelings are so much different from nearly anything ever encountered in civilian life. Trust me if you have not been there; it's very different.

Beyond the relationships among your friends and peers, there are the relationships that must be established between yourself and your subordinates and between yourself and your superiors. Again, those are relationships that may have some similarities with those in civilian life, but the results of those relationships have much more severe consequences in military life. In civilian life, if you do not follow the directives of your superiors, the consequences could be as severe as termination of your employment. In the military, the results can be much more significant, and, yes, there are exceptions in civilian life that have similarities, particularly in law-enforcement and fire fighting. Disobeying direct orders in the military is a court-martial offense, and doing so could very well cause others to lose their lives or fail in a critical mission, which could lead to a tremendous loss of life for your own forces or allied forces. Then termination of employment with a less than honorable discharge from the military service can be the final result, and that will follow you for the rest of your life.

The relationship between yourself and your superiors is one of great complexity. Your superiors are there to give you direction and guidance; not any different from civilian life, right? Well, not quite right. In most cases in civilian life you may well have the option of questioning the guidance that your superiors give you and even sit down to discuss the matter intelligently. However, in the military, and especially in a combat situation, if you hesitate in reacting to a direct order, people may well die as a result. If that were to be the case, then the person who questioned the direct order would be guilty of disobeying a direct order.

The bottom line is we may not like or even respect the individual appointed over us, but we must respect the rank and position of the person. We may not agree with the decisions he or she makes, but as long as the decision is lawful, it must be complied with completely. However, if the order is not a lawful order and it is obvious that it would involve wrongdoing on the part of others, then and only then can the order be dismissed and not complied with. Sometimes there is a rather fine line between lawful and unlawful orders, and nobody ever wants to be confronted with such a decision. Consequently, many have been coerced into following unlawful orders and they find themselves in more trouble than the person giving the unlawful order in the first place. There are situations now and then where one must merely let his conscience be his guide.

One good example of a misinterpretation of orders from the Vietnam War archives would be the infamous My Lai massacre, which occurred in March of 1968. At the very foundation of this incident there was an order given to destroy the village of My Lai, which in itself was nothing unlawful. The village was in what was considered a hostile area, around which it was presumed there were no friendly people. The village should not have been occupied at all, let alone by friendly people. The presumption was not correct, and several hundred civilians were killed, including women and children.

US Army Lieutenant William Calley was the platoon leader on the ground at the time. Captain Earnest Medina gave him the order to destroy the village, which would normally just involve burning it to the ground. Another presumption would have been that the village was being used as a sanctuary for the Viet Cong or North Vietnamese Army (NVA) troops. Something went horribly wrong somewhere in the process, and that has never been made clear.

More than just "torching" the village occurred. Those who were involved in the operation were probably hoping, possibly presuming, that there would be no civilians actually occupying the village, but that was not the case. All of the people of the village were gathered together, lined up and shot to death, and buried in a shallow ditch. Only one man was held responsible for this horrible atrocity; William Calley. The specifics of the orders given remain a mystery. In whatever manner he may have interpreted the order to destroy the village, it could not have included killing all of the civilians, unless he was told specifically to do so, and that, of course, would not have been a lawful order, and that would have been one to dismiss. It was determined that Lt. Calley took the initiative to perpetrate the crime, and he was convicted. No one else faced any charges, even though several up the chain of command probably should have shared in the responsibility. We are all responsible for our own actions, or lack thereof. No others in this case were held responsible for any actions they may have taken, and yet there had to have been others involved.

The subject at hand is the subordinate-superior relationship, and I cannot help but use a personal example, because it illustrates perfectly what we're dealing with. This one begins with an operation initiated by all the activities going on during the Tet '68 offensive in South Vietnam with my unit operating in the surrounding areas of Saigon. It is a situation that could occur anywhere at any time, not at all unique to the war in Vietnam. The mission of my unit, the 199th Light Infantry Brigade (LIB), included guarding the southern approaches to Saigon. My platoon was given an extremely simple and routine mission to patrol and check out activities in the southern outskirts of the city. We were only to observe what was going on and report what we saw. In that respect, it was more of a reconnaissance mission.

We began our patrol at the southern part of a road leading north into the city. We were to proceed north for a kilometer or so, turn right at a major intersection, continuing for approximately another thousand meters and make another right, heading south, and then returning to our base of operations. It all sounds pretty simple, right? I always remember the old Jell-O commercial on television, which ended with, "All that wiggles is not Jell-O." What a wonderful analogy, the concept of which certainly never occurred to me as a dumb kid. However, later in life, as a less dumb adult, I have been able to apply that concept to a tremendous number of situations, where things do not turn out to be what you imagined them to be.

We headed north from our starting point and found that all along the left flank of our designated route everything seemed quite normal, in that there were normal activities among the people; motor vehicles, mopeds, bicycles and pedestrians all seemed to be moving along and milling about with absolutely nothing interfering with what one might expect on a typical day in Saigon. We reached the intersection where we were to turn right and head east on the north leg of our route. We noticed exactly the same things going on along that segment of the route; nothing out of the ordinary. We were not doing house-to-house searches; we were merely observing of all activities along the route, looking for anything that might seem unusual for that area.

We came to the last intersection, where we were to head back south and return to our base camp. After a short distance, it occurred to us that the situation had changed rather remarkably and abruptly. Activity in this area was not only abnormal, but had ceased entirely. All traffic disappeared; no vehicles, no people. There was nothing but an eerie silence.

At this point I instructed all of my squads to proceed much more slowly and cautiously, looking carefully into every house and building along the way. As we proceeded down the street, we noticed a canal on our left flank. A hundred meters or so to the south, on the far side of the canal, was a Vietnamese P.F. (Popular Forces) camp. The Popular Forces were similar to our state National Guard forces; citizen soldiers. As we continued further, we noticed that ahead of us was a barricade across the road. It was composed of a variety of junk, stacked high and wrapped with barbed wire.

We proceeded down the road, closer to the barricade. The PF soldiers, observing our approach, began to call out to us in broken English from across the canal, "No further, G.I.; beaucoup (always pronounced by the Vietnamese, and American troops bookoo) VC" They were giving us warnings that could not have been misunderstood. It was very clear to me that there was a whole bunch of bad guys to my front. I had a few options at my disposal, but, silly as it may seem now, I opted for doing things the "right" way. I brought my company commander up on the radio and requested permission to recon by fire. That merely meant that I wanted to open up with small arms fire, and see what I might receive in return, thereby identifying enemy targets and taking the offensive at that point.

What was the response to my request? "Negative!" I immediately came back with, "Say again, over."

"Negative on that request. There may be innocent civilians in the area," he responded.

I was dumbfounded. I came back with, "Six (Six being the commander's designation or call sign), let me make myself perfectly clear. I have friendlies to my left who have told me very clearly that there are Victor Charlies to my front on the other side of the barrier." Victor Charlie was the name we always used for Viet Cong or VC. I continued with my request. "Now, once again, request permission to recon by fire! Over."

"Three-six, this is six. I say again, Lieutenant, (a very significant breach in communications security) permission denied! Consider this a direct order. Proceed forward until you make contact. Do you roger that?"

"Affirmative, six, but a couple more requests: Have med-evac on-call, as we will take casualties. Also, request that you too be on-call, as I am quite sure we will need assistance. Over."

"Roger that. Will be ready to assist. Out."

Well, there I was with a "direct order" for what I considered a potential suicide mission from a company commander for whom I had little or no respect (and we were both of the same rank, first lieutenants, he ranking me by about three months). I then initiated "my plan."

As soon as I had my first three people across the barrier, all hell broke loose with small arms and automatic weapons fire, grenades and RPGs (rocket-propelled grenades). All three men who had maneuvered across the barrier were wounded and needed immediate extraction and medical evacuation. That, however, did not happen immediately. We were all pinned down with little to no ability to move without being cut to pieces. Somehow, in the midst of all that chaos, we managed to get the wounded to safety and eventually evacuated. While all this was going on, I was able to return to my company commander by radio, to inform him of the situation. He assured me that he was on his way with the remainder of the company. I waited for a painfully long time while the situation worsened and became critical.

Although some specific details are hazy, somewhere amid all the confusion, during this rather hellacious firefight, an RPG round quickly caught my eye a second before it exploded only three to four feet from me, sending me ten or fifteen feet through the air. After recovering myself, taking an inventory of all my arms, legs, fingers, and other body parts, I discovered that I miraculously did not have a drop of blood flowing from my body. I was amazed at being unscathed by that one, and continued the mission.

I thanked the Lord for having my guardian angel looking after me once again, as well as those men who were in close proximity to me. It seems like it must have taken a whole legion of guardian angels to look after me while I was over there. I was prone to being in the wrong places at the wrong times. It tended to happen quite regularly. At the same time, I have to remind myself that I was the platoon leader, and, as such, was, as my old OCS instructors used to tell us (students), a prime target for enemy fire.

While all this was going on, and I still had neither seen nor heard from my company commander, I was finally able to bring him back up on the "horn" to find out where he was. Of course, he was pinned down, having run into the main force of the VC element. In actuality, these bad boys were no longer Viet Cong, who were mainly local guerillas, sympathetic to the North Vietnamese cause; they were NVA regulars. My rescuers had been ambushed and were now immobile! Needless to say, but, of course, I'll say it anyway, I had mixed emotions on that one.

The end result was that a tank company came to our rescue and leveled that part of the town with their main guns and 50-caliber machine guns. I am not at all certain of it, but we may well have lost a few "innocent" civilians during that little skirmish. I learned later that five or six additional infantry battalions, along with the tank company, came to join in the "fun" that day. All of that, and I was not initially allowed to recon by fire. What more can I say? Well, I can say one more thing. For what turned into a major battle, my platoon and I just happened to be the unit to initiate that whole mess. I could ask, "Why me, Lord?" Then again, I have already said that I had a bad habit of being in the wrong places at the wrong times. Hey, apparently, it was another victory for our side; so, who should complain? I still do, however, because some of my guys were hurt, and I always hated that part worse than anything else. Anyway, so much for the relationship between my commander and me. We did not see eye to eye, but I was forced to take his orders whether I liked it or not. That is the name of the game.

Like the relationship between you and your superiors, the relationship between you and your subordinates is equally important to understand. As you progress through all of your training cycles, including basic training and advanced training, you will have made many close friends, having lived with them, trained with them, eaten, showered, and suffered in every conceivable way with them for fourteen to sixteen weeks. You will feel closer to some of them than you have ever felt about anyone in your entire life. They are now a very big part of your life. You may one day be relying upon one another to stay alive. It is really a different relationship than what most people have ever encountered.

If your rank is an E-4, or even an E-3 in the enlisted ranks (the lowest enlisted rank being E-1), you could have four or five people within your realm of responsibility. Now, these people certainly can still be your friends, but in a tactical environment the relationship goes a bit further. Whatever these people are doing is suddenly your business, whether you want it to be or not. If they are doing the right things, you get the credit; if they are doing the wrong things, you still get the credit, but it's now called blame. You have passed into the zone of leadership and you now have the responsibility of leading people, and you had better know a little bit more than the people you are leading if you wish to be successful.

Rank, and, therefore, leadership responsibilities, can come quickly in the military, as your superiors are always watching for men and women with leadership potential. If you demonstrate that potential, then, as soon as you meet the minimum requirements for the next rank and pay grade and pass a promotion board, promotion should be the next step. I am quite sure that many of you can look back and find a few exceptions to that generality, and I can too, but hopefully that remains to be one of our goals.

During times of war or national emergencies those promotions can happen faster than you can imagine, and even faster than what you might be able to prepare for. Often people are promoted before they are mentally, emotionally, or even academically capable of accepting a new level of responsibility. There are times unfortunately when leaders are wounded or even killed in action, and someone has to take their place, regardless of rank or experience. That someone may be very low ranking, but a superior has seen enough potential in him to place him in that leadership role by necessity.

In my case, I enlisted in the Army and only achieved an E-3 pay grade before entering my OCS class. In the meantime, however, while awaiting my OCS class date, because I had prior experience in high school and college ROTC, and having been a student platoon leader in my basic training and my advanced infantry training, I became what was called an "acting jack" (which means I wore the temporary rank of a sergeant E-5), but was still paid my E-3 salary.

I was pushing troops for several months at Fort Ord, California, near Monterey. Regardless of what the Army was paying me, I had the responsibility of two pay grades higher than I was. It worked out very well for me, however, as it was great training for what I was trying to do. I could have all the leadership schools the Army has to offer, but this was great on-the-job training that could not be beat. Some do not perform well being abruptly placed in that situation, but I did quite well, having been adequately prepared. One of my sons, Brent, who never went over E-4 in rank, was placed in charge of a whole motor pool in Afghanistan, which was a sergeant E-6 pay slot, and he did perfectly well. Again, he had a great deal more responsibility to accept than that for which he was being paid, but it was great experience, and helped him out later in life. He is thankful for it today.

After completing Infantry OCS at the rank of second lieutenant, as well as it being a time of war, with the Vietnam War well underway, promotions came fast. From second lieutenant to first lieutenant was one year, and from first lieutenant to captain was another year. I knew a young man while I was in Korea who was a captain in the Army and was not legally old enough to drink. Many people are not able to acquire that kind of rank in that short period of time without position and responsibility going straight to their heads. Of course, there are those who, regardless of age, can't handle it anyway. We've all run into that type of person before.

Those who cannot handle the responsibilities of leadership are simply bad leaders. They are found in every walk of life and most of the time we just have to deal with them the best we know how. Somehow they have managed to work their way through the promotions without their weaknesses being detected. Now that does not really seem all that different from civilian life, does it? We always like to think that those "bad apples" will be weeded out through a natural process, but reality strikes and we find that it does not always happen. In any case, we can see that growth and maturity develop at different levels for each of us, and sometimes it seems not to happen at all.

# Chapter 4 – Stress: Absolutely Critical

As each person progresses through his or her career, be it short or full-term, he naturally begins to develop a knack for organizational skills, a necessity for anyone in the military. Long before one even begins to assume leadership responsibilities, he has personal equipment to take care of, schedules to keep, appointments to make, and it may be the first time in his life that he does not have any parents to look after him to make sure he meets all of his responsibilities. He may well have a drill sergeant breathing down his neck, but he still has to be able to function on his own in order to be successful. He finds himself becoming more and more organized as time goes on, and more than likely doesn't even realize it.

In the beginning it is only the soldier's, sailor's or airman's personal life that he must keep in order, and then it begins to encompass others as he becomes responsible for the lives of the very people he has been around for such a long time. His horizons are expanded, and he will begin to feel more and more self-worth. There are others who are now relying upon him for assistance in developing their own skills. Leaders emerge through a natural process. Becoming a natural leader with an assertive personality, he is able to develop his natural skills further through continued training and continued study in history, leadership and academic subjects pertaining to his own specialty skills, as well as other subjects connected to the military in general.

As promotions continue, so do the levels of responsibility and the number of people for whom that person is responsible. Organizational skills become increasingly important as the sizes of the units of which the person is in charge increase. It is one thing being in charge of a five- or six-man fire team, and quite another being in charge of an Army division of six or eight thousand people. Most end up somewhere in between, but the concept remains the same. Without a good sense of organization there will never be success in whatever the endeavor.

It goes with the territory that along with added responsibilities comes added stress. Stress can, of course, be good at manageable levels, but then, when it goes the other way, life can become uncomfortable. Stress can build character; it can also tear it apart. We all have to learn to live with it and accept it as an old friend. If it were not for a bit of stress in our lives, we would probably never grow mentally, emotionally and psychologically. That concept is at the heart of all leadership schools in the military. They all place emphasis on forcing the individual to work under maximum levels of stress. More often than not, this is perceived as one of the negatives of leadership training, but, if people can learn to work under extreme stress, then they will probably be able to function well under the extreme stresses of combat, and that is the ultimate goal of becoming an effective military leader.

The fact that every day in a combat environment brings normal stress does not need to be emphasized here, but now and then situations emerge and surpass those routine daily anxieties. I once experienced a situation that could very well apply to anyone in a combat area anywhere in the world, and one that has probably recurred many times over in the history of war. My platoon and I came under a 122mm rocket attack. It was an occasion for which all my background in stress training came to the surface and, in retrospect, was undoubtedly responsible for saving my life and perhaps the lives of several others.

Before charging into the incident itself, an explanation of what led up to it and the actual cause of it is probably in order. Living in the village of Lang Duk, our company personnel became familiar with many of the local inhabitants. Two men in my platoon became very close to a couple of sisters in the village. In fact, they became girlfriends and boyfriends. The girls were truly beautiful young ladies, being a mixture of Vietnamese and French.

One day an open Jeep carrying two South Vietnamese National Police officers drove into the village, and the first thing that caught their attention was the two sisters who were just standing around talking. The police immediately drove up to the girls and were about to arrest them for prostitution. I saw what was happening and headed in that direction.

The police spoke and understood English very well, and I told them that I knew the girls and would vouch for them, and they were not prostitutes. The police were determined to arrest the girls anyway, and I, of course, protested. I knew at that point that the police officers only wanted the girls for themselves, and it was not difficult to imagine what would have happened to them. Tension increased between the officers and me, and I ended up pulling out the .45 caliber automatic I had holstered, put it to the driver's head and told him to leave before I had to blow his brains out. The officers were not at all pleased with that development, but they did reluctantly depart from the village, giving me "the evil eye" as they drove off.

The following night, with the exception of a few routine patrols that were out, my company was not engaged in any operation, and we were still in our village base camp. I, two other lieutenants, several NCO's, along with other enlisted men and, I believe, the same two girls mentioned above, were all in one of the hooches (thatched huts) playing cards. We were all very casual, as we were expecting nothing significant to happen that night. There had been no intelligence reports of any hostile forces in the area. I did not even have my boots on; I was wearing plastic Vietnamese sandals. Suddenly one of the loudest and most mind-boggling explosions any of us had ever encountered went off, seemingly right next to us. We all froze in a minor state of shock, having no idea what had just happened. Not more than ten seconds later another round came "screaming" in and exploded. That one was definitely a motivation to move. I directed everyone to run to the nearest bunker, not more than fifteen or twenty meters away.

We all "hunkered down" within the bunker to await any further in-coming rounds. Sure enough, the third round came in and, astonishingly, it was a direct hit on the hooch in which we had moments before been playing cards. Had we still been there, it is likely we all would have been killed. It would also have altered history somewhat, as my three sons would not be here today, not to mention the families of all the others. About three more rounds came in, and I was thinking that each of those rounds was getting closer and closer to our position. Although I also thought that it could well have been my imagination, I was not going to take any chances. I directed everyone to run as fast as their legs could move them down to the next bunker, about forty or fifty meters away. After the first two steps I was barefoot, as my plastic sandals stuck six to eight inches deep in the mud dike. That did not slow me down, however. I kept right on "truckin'."

We arrived at the next position just in time for the next round to hit, followed by about three more after that. Then it was all over, except for the utter chaos going on in the village. There were flames shooting fifty to a hundred feet into the night sky from all of the grass hooches that had sustained hits or near hits and had burst into flames. There were women and children running around screaming at the top of their lungs, with sheer terror in their eyes. I seriously doubt that any of them had any idea what was happening to them, as to my knowledge, this was the only time rockets had ever hit their village. A good portion of their village had been destroyed and there were friends or family members who had been badly injured or killed, and this was scaring the daylights out of them. This could most assuredly be considered a high-stress situation. It was definitely the stress that caused me to make the seemingly mindless decisions to keep moving.

It was probably three or four years later, that I took a closer look at the slides that I had taken the next morning of the results of the attack, and came to the conclusion that the people who were firing the rockets at us were actually directing that fire and correcting fire as they continued to shoot. The first bunker that we were in took a direct hit. I could see plainly in one of those slides a corner of the bunker blown away, along with debris scattered around the front of the bunker. If you are keeping track, that would be two direct hits on locations that were previously occupied by the others and myself. Those bad boys must have run out of ammunition before they were able to zero in on us again. That phenomenal attack only took one life and injured two others, all of whom were Vietnamese civilians, not to downplay the serious nature of those losses. However, none of my people were even injured, miraculous as that may seem, and it certainly did seem that way to me.

My personal conclusion was that the two policemen I encountered the previous day were directly responsible for that attack. It was just another example of not knowing the "good guys" from the "bad guys," something that we always faced in that war, and that situation has not changed today in the Middle East. It makes our rules of engagement difficult to enforce under such circumstances.

There are so many bizarre incidents that occurred throughout my own combat experiences that it is difficult to remember all of them. There are always some, of course, that never disappear from even fading memories like my own. One of the most interesting and, indeed, most bizarre incidents involved one of my young platoon headquarters men, my own RTO (radio-telephone operator).

One of the most difficult, and, I should add, most stressful things that can happen to any leader in combat is when one or more of his people is injured or in a worst case scenario killed. The one thing he continuously tries to do is keep his people as safe as possible. Sometimes it just does not work out as well as planned. In those situations a leader recognizes the phenomenal differences in people, particularly in the way that they react so differently to situations – physically, mentally, emotionally and even spiritually.

My company was again on a routine patrol in the Mekong Delta. While crossing a large, open rice paddy, we came under fire from a nearby grove of nippa-palm, right where "Charlie" used to love to hide out in ambush. "Charlie" was directing effective fire on us, and we were pretty well pinned down. We called in some of our direct-support artillery to help us out, and then I decided that we should incorporate some good old-fashioned, conventional fire and maneuver by fire-teams. That is where a fire team, or half of a squad, lays a base of fire, while the other team moves forward. Then they change over, and the first team lays a base of fire while the other moves. It seemed to work well for us until it came time for my platoon headquarters element to move.

We had one of our fire teams laying a base of fire, and I started to get up, yelling, "Okay, let's go!" My RTO (radio telephone operator), Courtney, called Corky by his friends, just lay there, eyes wide open, but motionless.

"Courtney! Get up, man! Move! What the hell's the matter with you? Get up!" He looked up at me slowly and calmly, with a rather hollow expression, and said, "Sir, I think I've been shot."

"What?" I blared out, in disbelief at what I was hearing. "What do you mean, you think you've been shot? You've either been shot or you haven't been shot. What makes you think you've been shot?" I suppose that was not the most intelligent question I have ever asked, though it did seem like he should have known one way or another.

I noticed blood on his shirt and helped him pull his shirt up, and, sure enough, blood was running out of a hole in the left side of his stomach. Easing him over to his side, I noticed that he had an exit wound on the same side through his back. The bullet had made a clean sweep through his body, not hitting a single vital organ. It passed through him almost without his even knowing it, except that his body did not want to move when I gave the command to do so. I might add that I did not consider that to be disobeying a direct order.

The point of the above incident is that, not only was it a very stressful situation that we all had to deal with, but to show that when some people are injured, they have such a low pain tolerance they scream "bloody murder," suffering tremendously. Others, who might sustain similar injuries, might feel very little pain. Their bodies go into a type of shock whereby the pain all but disappears. I am in that category myself. I have sustained some significant injuries in my life, and each time the pain I have experienced has been minimal. I am not at all sure whether that is good or bad, but it is a fact, and something we always have to be aware of in order to make the best decisions. We cannot base our decisions on the volume of the screams we hear. Unfortunately, the louder a wounded soldier tends to be on the battlefield, the more stress there can be among the troops. This can result in an individual making wrong decisions in times of crisis.

When it comes to dealing with the mental stresses of combat, there are some similarities to dealing with the physical elements. We all deal with situations differently from one another. What is now identified as post-traumatic stress disorder (PTSD), or, prior to Vietnam, as battle fatigue, does not apply to all who have experienced similar levels of combat stress. The vast majority of people who returned from Vietnam, and experienced a great deal of combat stress, have been perfectly all right without visible ill effects. I am thankful that I am among those.

Granted, there have been many who returned and experienced bad dreams, "flashbacks," depression and other related symptoms, but they are in the minority. Some have blamed addictions to alcohol and drugs on their combat experiences, but really, let's be honest about it. Can we not justify our weaknesses by blaming some negative, even traumatic experiences that we have not handled well? That is indeed a broad generality. I am quite aware that PTSD is real and valid for many, and probably many of my readers. Please do not take any of my comments personally. These are only my personal observations and conclusions that only apply to some. I am not a physician and would never make such a claim.

I can't help but think of a late friend of mine who was mentally ill, and a Vietnam veteran. He had continuing dreams, flashbacks, and lengthy cycles of depression, including attempts at suicide. Eventually he was diagnosed as a manic depressive and institutionalized as a result. He blamed his condition on his experiences in Vietnam, and was receiving disability from VA for PTSD. Wait a minute now. This man was aboard a Navy ship in the South China Sea! One of his responsibilities was to push a button that would launch a nuclear warhead in the event of such a necessity. He was a low-ranking enlisted man with limited decision-making authority. If someone else up the chain of command were to have given him an order to push the button, then he would have had to do it. He never came close to receiving such an order. The stress of that possibility, however, may have pushed him over the edge, apparently way beyond his mental capacity.

By no means would I ever try to "toot my own horn" or boast in any way about my experiences in Vietnam. Nor would I intentionally compare myself to others who served faithfully in the war, such as my friend whose service I do honor and respect. My infantry experiences in combat, however, have given me memories that nothing will ever erase. My friend probably never heard or saw a hostile shot fired in the war. He never saw enemy or friendly troops lying dead or wounded in a rice paddy, and yet he was diagnosed as dysfunctional. I have no idea if any of his symptoms were present before his war experiences. I am quite sure that war experiences can push people who may already have problems over the edge and worsen an already chronic condition, as well as possibly being the cause of it. So, who am I or anyone else to be the judge? The fact remains that we are all different and react differently under stress. As leaders, we must be aware of that.

My feelings are as strong about people who bleed the government unjustifiably for conditions that are exaggerated or perhaps nonexistent as they are for people who deserve to be reimbursed for conditions they endured and for which they receive nothing. I am a person who recognizes that the world just "ain't fair!" I won't even try to justify or change that situation. It's a fact of life. We live with it every day. We can whine about it or we can get on with life, and that would include life in the military or in the civilian world. I would much prefer getting over the lack of fairness and move along. Oh, sure, I do my share of whining from time to time, but hopefully much more of getting on with the more important things in life and making the very best of it. It really is a good life for those who plan to make it that way.

Accidents would be another category of stress that perhaps few would consider as terribly relevant, but for a leader, injuries and even fatalities as a result of accidents can be traumatic, even in peacetime. Not all injuries and fatalities sustained in war are a result of hostilities or interaction with the "bad guys." Sometimes things just happen, and sometimes people make them happen, intentionally or otherwise. Let's look at some possible scenarios that could very well be real today or could have been real in any war of the past.

Echo Company is on the move, hacking its way through thick jungle growth, or maybe just on the move across the desert, and they stop to take a quick break. After about fifteen minutes they get ready to pull out again and resume their advance. Now, keeping in mind that each man is well trained with his individual weapon, not only in firing that weapon, but also in maintaining it, and being more than moderately familiar with all safety precautions pertaining to that weapon, it is, nevertheless, possible that accidents can still happen. A complete and total imbecile knows that pulling on the trigger of a weapon with a round in the chamber, and the safety not engaged, will cause that weapon to discharge. Nevertheless, one of our young heroes, in getting up from the sitting position, grabs his rifle, with his right hand grasping the trigger housing, with his trigger finger on the trigger, of course, and the other hand grasping the upper portion of the barrel, left index finger over the muzzle of the weapon, proceeds to pull himself up to the standing position.

The rifle, of course, discharges and his left index finger disappears as one might expect. The question remains as to whether that incident is an accident or intentional. An injury such as that will definitely remove a man from the field. If he is intent enough upon doing that, possibly losing a finger is more appealing than the fear of possibly losing his life. Many have made such decisions. It is also virtually impossible to prove that such an occurrence is intentional, and no one ever tries. Although I presented that situation as hypothetical, it did indeed happen in my platoon in Vietnam.

Again, who is to say what constitutes an accident or an intentional deed? It probably helps to be a little crazy to make those kinds of bizarre decisions. I believe most people would rather take their chances with the enemy than to shoot themselves. If that man had made the decision to blow his finger off, then stress would without a doubt have been the cause of that incident. Whatever the case, losing a man from the field for any reason, without an immediate replacement, can cause stress to the leader and the remainder of the unit. After all, that is one more man short to accomplish the mission, and each individual is critical for every mission.

We all know, without being told, that a war zone can be dangerous. What might first come to mind is the fact that there are people out there trying to kill you, and, yes, I would certainly agree that is significant. However, it is also a fact that in wars in which Americans have fought, there have been significant numbers of non-hostile casualties, in addition to those caused by the enemy. According to "American War and Military Operations Casualties: Lists and Statistics," by Anne

Leland – Information Research Specialist and Mari-Jana "M-J" Oboroceana – Information Research Specialist, without running through all the statistics given, most of the wars and conflicts in which we have been involved show somewhere between twenty and forty percent of the total casualties to be non-hostile. Those numbers do include accidents.

The mere fact that the personal weapons we use in battle are extremely dangerous hopefully does not need mentioning. On the other hand, those who use them, as careful as we would all hope that they would be with them, do become a little careless from time to time, and accidents happen. I have had entirely too many such events happen to my soldiers.

One of the things that a commander or leader must always emphasize is using extreme caution when it comes to handling whatever weapon the individual is assigned. I again have to use one of my own examples here, as I did have an incident involving an M-79 grenade launcher while on an operation in Vietnam. Trying to instill maximum safety in all my men who carried that grenade launcher, I tried to keep them aware that the safety on the weapon was not effective, and we could not rely on it. Regardless of its effectiveness or ineffectiveness, I required that the operator always keep the safety on, and that, while walking, the breech (as it was a breech-loaded weapon) always be open, preferably without a round in the chamber. However, often it would be necessary to have the weapon loaded, particularly if we were in an extremely active and hostile area.

As often as I told my men repeatedly not to act like John Wayne, swinging the weapon back and forth Hollywood-style, with the right hand clutching the trigger housing, particularly with a round in the chamber, sure enough, here comes "the Duke," one of my grenadiers! On one forward swing of the weapon, his finger depressed the trigger, discharging the weapon. The round will not explode until it has traveled about fifty meters out. That part is the good news. The bad news is that the round struck the man in front of him, shattering the major bones in his right leg. The injured soldier was one more man I lost, never to see again, only because of carelessness. In this case, I could only accept the minor stress of the situation. The recipient of the M-79 round took the major stress, mostly physical in nature. The rest of us dealt with it the best we could. It's never a pretty picture.

I would say, since World War II, our greatest fears in combat have been the presence of snipers and booby traps, because, for both situations, there is seldom, if ever, any warning. That fact alone results in unending stress. One memory that will remain with me forever involved a booby trap, and it is one that all can identify with, particularly those who have been in a combat zone. It was one of those situations whereby we cannot seem to avoid the old cliché, "When you least expect it, expect it."

My company was going out to our relatively secure training area just outside of our village and base camp in order to practice tactical procedures. We proceeded out of the village in a single file with my platoon second in the line of march. The first platoon continued along the path without incident. Everyone in my platoon stayed in the same line of march until one man, four or five behind me, stepped a bit to the right side of the path and set off a pressure device which detonated an explosive, probably a mortar round, rigged as a booby trap. The explosion ripped the man's face off, leaving what appeared to be a slab of hamburger, but much more grotesque. A couple of others were also wounded, but not as seriously.

Looking at what was left of that poor, young man, I really thought that there was no way he could ever have survived such a traumatic injury. I thought he had taken his last breath. Amazingly enough, I heard later, well after his medical evacuation, that he survived, and that the doctors somehow put his face back together. I can only imagine what he must have looked like after all of his surgeries. I honestly do not recall what the man looked like before that incident. I never saw him again. I've seen disfigured men from the war and wondered if any of them could be the same man. I'll more than likely never know, as I have no idea today who the man was. He passed from me and my surroundings, but never from my memories. These kinds of events happen too frequently in war, and it is a continuing stress that endures without ceasing.

I mentioned snipers and that they are always among our greatest fears. It is not so much that they are extremely accurate in hitting their designated targets; it is the fact that someone is out there you cannot see, and he is attempting to place effective fire on you and your men, and there is little you can do about it. You can never see that little "bugger!" He may pop out of a very well camouflaged "spider hole." He may be hiding inside a grove of nippa-palm or he may be up on a nearby hilltop, or even in a tree. In any case, he can pin down a whole company of men, whereby no one can even maneuver on him, because they have no clue where he is. He can pick off several people before you have even a general idea of his direction, let alone his exact location. Oh, rest assured, they are very good at what they do. Let there be no doubt about that. We always have to presume that we have a formidable enemy, one for whom we should have a good deal of respect. I always did.

Most of the time sniper situations are taken seriously and can affect the whole nature of the mission, particularly when they slow you down and throw off the timing of the operation. Then again, there are times when it is not so much critical to the mission as it is harassing to groups or individuals. The example that follows could just as well be filed under humor, humility or lessons learned in how to avoid stressful situations. I must humbly apologize for using myself as an example so much, but I have been in so many of these situations that I cannot think of better examples than my own and they are universal in nature, in that they can apply to any combat environment and any time frame.

The first time I personally encountered a sniper was little more than a week after my arrival in Vietnam. After my initial briefing and a few hours of orientation to my new environment, I was assigned as a platoon leader in an infantry company. I was the new "green" second lieutenant; the "new kid on the block." Of course, the common term for those of us who had hardly enough time to see our first South Vietnamese sunset was the FNG's. The last two words of that abbreviation are new guys.

One critical element that probably should have been covered in my orientation, involved something as simple as the towels that I was carrying. All I brought with me on this little one-year adventure were some white towels that I had purchased at the Fort Polk, Louisiana exchange facility just before leaving the States. After a day or two with my unit, Alpha Company, 4th Battalion, 31st Infantry, 196th Light Infantry Brigade (L.I.B.), which was located on a hilltop a fair distance from a town called Chu Lai, it was time for a shower.

I stripped down, wrapped my white towel around my waist and proceeded off to the shower point, which was just a short hop across the company perimeter from my tent. About half way to the shower point, "Pop, pop, pop" rang out over my head. I dropped to my belly at a speed nearly matching the bullets passing over my head, and quickly began the old rapid low-crawl that I had learned so well throughout all of my previous, non-live-fire training. Somewhere along the way I left my white towel behind, but I was ever so happy to have my own behind still intact. I made it back to my tent, which was surrounded by sandbags about eighteen inches high. Needless to say, but, of course, per usual, I'll say it anyway, my next purchase at the local PX was two or three olive drab towels. Let us just call it another lesson learned, and I acquired new wisdom.

That same Viet Cong sniper who pinned me to the ground was one of our regulars. Even though he did single me out, I did not take my encounter with him all that personally, because I was not his only target. In fact, almost every night, close to our dinner hour, he would start firing up our perimeter. He was so regular that I later referred to him as "Five O'clock Charlie," in reference to the character in the old TV series, M*A*S*H who, although never seen, flew over the camp to drop his bomb every day at about five o'clock in the afternoon. I never took our sniper entirely seriously either, as he never seemed to be trying to hit anyone. I think he just liked the idea of harassing us more than anything. Hey, when the bullets are flying, so is the stress level, particularly when you are the target.

Another situation I encountered was with my next unit, Echo Company, 2nd Battalion, 3rd, Infantry, 199th Light Infantry Brigade, in the Mekong Delta, where I re-coined "Five O'clock Charlie." At this location we also had an uninvited dinner-hour guest who liked to harass us, but not a sniper. This time we had a mortar crew "out there" somewhere, who enjoyed dropping 60-millimeter mortar rounds through our perimeter each night, nearly always the same time. The rounds would start dropping at one end of the perimeter, and these guys would "walk" them right across to the other side; then it would stop. That would be it. As I recall, no one was ever injured, but we did have a few close calls, and, per usual, the stress factor would have a tendency to increase significantly, but only for a short time.

I remember one night, when the mortar rounds began falling, there was one young man seated atop our three-seat commode. He was in the process of his daily constitutional when the rounds began to fall. He tried desperately to dethrone himself as rapidly as possible, but one round landed very close to him, and the impact blew him off into the bushes. It was a rather messy situation, but he did survive it, untouched by mortar fragments. As "crappy" as that situation was, I'm sure that he was quite thankful for the result. I was not sure that story would be one of his favorite war stories to share with his children. I could be wrong, however. It is important to understand that near tragedies can become some of the best humor, but only when those would-be tragedies are averted.

Another near tragedy, as well as quite stressful occasion, comes to mind. Instantaneous reactions, when coming under enemy fire, can be crucial to survival. I can't tell you how many times, when coming under sniper fire or other enemy contact, I reacted so quickly that, as my body dropped to the ground, at what seemed the speed of lightning, my helmet remained in the air momentarily, later catching up to me, often abruptly, frequently giving me a significant headache. Well, a very close friend of mine, also an infantry platoon leader at the time, has, probably to this day, a souvenir he retained from a similar incident. His platoon came under attack, and automatic weapons fire came directly at him. He too took a quick dive for the ground. When he retrieved his helmet, he noticed that it had two clean holes, one through each side. Had his head been in the helmet at the moment of impact, he would have had a bullet through at least one of his temples. There is no doubt in my mind that souvenir has a good deal of value to him today. Yes, memories are made of this.

Frequently I refer to the fact that our units are, more often than not, out looking for the enemy until they find us. That is pretty much the nature of war. Both sides are out looking for one another, and both sides try to be prepared for when the other side finds them. Probably 90 percent of the time my unit was out on an offensive operation, it quickly turned into a defensive action, when we came under attack from an ambush. Our ever-so cunning enemy would be in position, just waiting for our approach or advance. On one such occasion we all knew there were enemy (in our case Viet Cong) in the area. We just had no idea how many there were or where they might be. They were, per usual, out there somewhere, and we were to progress until we made contact, whatever that might mean.

Sure enough, on this day we did make contact and were able to figure out what it all meant. What a wonderful education we were given, compliments of the NVA. We came under fire from automatic and semi-automatic weapons, as well as RPG's. We were pinned down. The first line of defense would be to call in the "big boys," i.e., artillery, and in this case we also had resources with which to call in air strikes from the Air Force. In addition, we had helicopter gunships at our disposal. We used everything we had, and to add a personal touch, we used our 81mm mortars. We estimated that there was a platoon-size unit in front of us. We never knew how many there were, as they were more than adequately concealed inside a nippa-palm grove, and we could seldom see what we were shooting at unless they were right in front of us.

We continued to pound the area for a good twenty or thirty minutes. By the time all of that heavy-duty support was through with their fire missions, added to our own assets, you would think that not even a rat would have been alive. Life is full of surprises. We felt perfectly comfortable initiating our assault on the enemy. After all of that unbelievable pounding, we still were fired upon from every direction. It was absolutely phenomenal what our enemy could withstand and still be ready to fight. Very frequently, and it was the case this time, we found that they were all underground, easily avoiding our rather ruthless assault. We frequently found their underground tunnel systems to be extremely elaborate.

Well, we did manage to prevail with minimal casualties and we were able to overrun their position. It was still tough to tell how many of them there were. We could only count the dead. The rest of them disappeared into the "bush." I probably should say that most of them disappeared, because, as my platoon continued to advance, we came under fire from a bomb crater to our front, which had been created by the previous air strike. The shooter seemed to be alone, but he was putting effective fire on us.

One of my young heroes decided to take the initiative to get close enough to the shooter to toss a hand-grenade into the hole. It seemed like a good idea at the time. Well, much to our chagrin, out of that same hole, which was about three quarters full of water, came the same grenade, which my main man had just thrown. Our adversary picked it up and threw it right back in our direction. There was no time to think about our next plan; we hit the dirt, trying to disappear under our helmets, and, of course, saying some quick prayers. Surprising as it may seem, no one was hit by the fragments, as it exploded right in the middle of us. As much as the stress level diminished at that point, our adversary still seemed to be a significant threat.

With a couple of percussion grenades hanging on my web gear, I decided it was my responsibility, and in all of our best interests, to get rid of this character. The percussion grenades are different from regular fragmentation grenades (frags). They are not metal and do not scatter metal fragments. They are made with a high explosive and, therefore, cause a concussive shock.

I crawled carefully toward the hole with several of my men covering me. I pulled the pin, released the handle, igniting the fuse, and waited. Most fuses on grenades are set for about four and a half to five seconds before detonation. I held it for three and a half to four seconds, praying that it would not be one of those short fuses, and threw it into the hole. That technique is called "cooking it off," the idea of which is to prohibit the bad guy from picking it up and throwing it back at you, as had just happened. Those few seconds of cook-off time do not help the stress level. It detonated almost immediately, as planned, and I again, of course, thanked the Lord for that. Just to make sure that our little friend did not survive and have other plans in mind, I unloaded a twenty-round magazine of my CAR-15 (my personal weapon) into the hole. He did not come forward again, and we continued our mission.

I suppose I cannot depart from the subject of stress without at least mentioning an incident that was perhaps the most stressful moment of my life, and more than likely in the lives of many others, and it occurred in that same area of the world. My company was once again on a rather lengthy operation in the Mekong Delta, and we had been in contact (engaged with the enemy) for most of the day. We had broken contact in the afternoon, and were ready to think about where to stop for the night. We were in the middle of hostile territory with enemy forces all around us, and yet we still had to stop for the night.

A location was selected for our night position. I have no idea at what level the decision was made, but that decision was absolutely ridiculous. There is no way I would ever have picked such a place to spend the night. It was right in the middle of a rice paddy, which left us completely open to attack. There were open fields of fire in nearly every direction, which was actually to our advantage, but the bad part was that we were extremely vulnerable. We were the proverbial "sitting ducks." We had rolls of concertina wire sent out to us so we could establish a more secure perimeter, since we anticipated the possibility of major problems. As it became dark, the weather took a change for the worse. It began to rain and continued throughout the night.

As night turned into early morning, one of the most logical times for VC or NVA attacks, sure enough, the inevitable occurred. The ideal conditions of darkness and bad weather materialized, and they took advantage of it. They executed a massive early morning attack. Breaking through the torrential rain and the darkness were sudden bursts of automatic weapons fire, seemingly from everywhere, and explosions outside and within our perimeter, both enemy and friendly. With each flash of an explosion, there were silhouettes of enemy soldiers projected onto our pupils. I could not recall ever having seen so many enemy soldiers attacking our position all at the same time. It was mind-boggling.

Lying in open rice paddies with that flood of rain coming down, we were all in water up to our necks, firing over the mud dykes in front of us, most of the time not even seeing our targets. In the midst of the firefight an RPG rocket swished in right between me and my platoon sergeant, Sergeant Joe Terrell, and stuck in the side of the mud dike about three feet away from both of our heads. This was the second time I had come that close to an RPG round, but this one did not detonate. With the one that went off I had no time to think about it. It happened so quickly that it was all over almost before it started.

This time there were two of us, and we had time just to look at the round sticking in the mud, right in front of our faces, wondering at what moment the delayed fuse might ignite and take us with it. Well, I'm very happy to say, it never did go off, but for several moments we had to think about taking our final breaths, though in reality neither of us was probably even breathing. I'm fairly certain that I was holding my breath. That was scary. I am the first to admit my stress level was about as high as it could possibly be.

Most of the above situations involve developing the ability to deal with stress. In the same context, during many of those stressful times, we are also required to make some critical decisions; decisions that affect the people with whom we work, and decisions which could mean life or death for those who are directly affected by them. When a team leader or a major unit commander decides to make a move, be it moving three or four people twenty meters or a division commander moving his unit fifty kilometers, each phase of that move could put our troops into a deadly situation, perhaps walking into an ambush or coming across a major enemy offensive. People may die as a direct result of that one decision.

Each person must ask himself if he is able to deal with the results of the decisions he makes. Sometimes things happen that are inevitable. One might have made the only logical decision that could possibly have been made, and people still die. The decision maker must be of a mindset that, if he or she has made a good decision based on all of the immediately available information, then the result of the decision could well just be left to fate. He has done the best he knows how and has to be able to deal with the end result. A good decision is a good decision, regardless of the end result. Now and then things just go badly without anyone being at fault.

Although my observations could constitute a rather broad generality, and there could be many exceptions, I have noticed in the military that, as individual growth continues, and it always will, regardless of age, rank or experience, the skill of decision making improves, unless dementia or something of that nature occurs first. The more a person is immersed in the process, the more those skills will be developed.

Most have heard the term "born leader." I am not at all convinced that such a person has ever existed. There are undoubtedly personality types that would be more conducive to leading rather than following. The more assertive or extraverted person is going to be more prone to take charge than the non-assertive or introverted person. However, for those who become good leaders, those skills are a long time in the making. They take a great deal of knowledge, training and experience to master. It does not happen overnight. It has also been said more than once that to be a good leader you must first be a good follower.

Sometimes, though it may not be entirely accurate, it is fun to try to analyze our own personalities to some degree. Imagine yourself in a situation where you are forced to make a financial decision, such as buying a new car. There are those who might take two months looking at all the details of a particular car; not just the specifications on the car, but the Consumer Reports recommendations, car magazine articles and whatever else is available to them. My wife is in that category. Another person might walk right up to the same car and buy it on the spot, driving it off the showroom floor. I have done that before. Some might call me an impulsive buyer. Maybe, but I prefer to think of myself as being decisive. Most of the time being impulsive implies something negative, as though the person has not put nearly enough thought into the matter. I look at it a little differently. Where many people may take the whole two months to decide on that car, I will, nine times out of ten, go to a car lot, pick out the one I want and drive away with it. That would be without the "help" of my wife. I prefer impulsive buying, which only means that the decision is made much more quickly. That has to result from my extensive military background. I am definitely a product of my environment.

Every individual who has had even a short career in the military will take home a level of decisiveness that he probably never had before those experiences. It is the nature of the military life. We can all look around and observe the people with whom we come into contact daily. It is not difficult to figure out which ones have had prior military experience. Just what is it that makes them stand out among all the others? Well, there might be a certain bearing that makes them physically stand out, which would probably include their posture, but the one thing that may well single them out is the fact that they usually want to be involved in the decision-making process. They are generally the take-charge type of people. They seem to have a certain confidence that most people do not naturally possess.

That obvious confidence is just another benefit most can assume from the military experience. At the same time I would not want to imply that those without military experience could not possess some of the same qualities, but those qualities do predominate among military people. When I speak of military people, I speak of present, as well as past military. The Marines say, "Once a Marine, always a Marine." The same can be said of all branches of service. It is in your blood to stay. You can watch some of today's "reality" shows on television and observe how some of the personality characteristics of the participants are consistent with their experiences. It is usually easy to tell those who have had a military background.

The element of decisiveness ties directly to that of problem solving, which is merely a process of collecting facts about a difficult situation, eliminating everything that will not help to solve that dilemma, and finally incorporating all that will contribute to finding a solution. At that point you have simplified the whole process, and what you are left with is nothing but all of the positive elements with which to find the solution. The only thing left is deciding which one will work out best after taking all factors into consideration. That, admittedly, over-simplifies the process, but let's lay out a problem and put it to the test, utilizing the above process.

Let's put ourselves into an infantry environment. Stay with me, both ladies and gentlemen, as the principles remain the same for nearly all situations. You are an infantry platoon leader, and, yes, today you can be a man or a woman. You have a thirty-man platoon, not completely up to strength, but able to function efficiently (normal for a wartime scenario). Your platoon is out on a mission, not necessarily to engage with the enemy, but just to find out who is out there, collect as much intelligence information as possible and report the results. Of course, your comment might well be, "Hey, we're not a long range patrol or a special operations unit. We're just a bunch of grunts." Don't worry about it. Bear with me and let's keep playing out the problem.

All right, we are moving across an open field, as we would have to go several kilometers out of our way to avoid it and we do not have that kind of time. We are widely spread out in the most advantageous tactical formation to cover ourselves from the front and flanks. Approaching the end of the wide clearing, we come under automatic weapons fire and RPG rounds zeroing in at us. The automatic weapons fire is coming from three directions and the RPG rounds are coming from two directions; the right front and the left front. Within minutes you have two wounded people who need immediate medical evacuations, and one KIA. You and your platoon are completely pinned down and are unable to move without sustaining more casualties. What are you going to do now?

Are you going to develop the situation further and eliminate the enemy if possible, break contact and get the heck out of there before the enemy is able to gather more information about you than you should ever allow him, or somehow try to continue on to complete your original mission? What are you going to do, Lieutenant? What is your first step?

What did we say? Gather the facts. 1.) Our unit is in the open. 2.) We have small arms, automatic weapons and RPG rounds coming in at us from several directions. 3.) We have two wounded and one dead. 4.) We are pinned down and unable to move without sustaining more casualties.

What are our options? 1.) To break off and vacate the area. 2.) Stay and fight. There appear to be no other options. Trying to break off would undoubtedly be catastrophic, compounding the problem of the dead and wounded. We have no choice but to stay and fight. We don't know exactly who or how many bad guys are out there, but we do know where they are.

The first option that should come to mind is indirect fire. The target is too formidable for our own mortars. So our direct support artillery is the first possible solution to the problem. That should hopefully suppress the fire, take many of them out, and possibly enable you to either move in and finish the job or move back to take care of the dead and wounded, particularly the latter.

If the artillery is effective, and the enemy breaks off, then you can move some of your people forward and complete your mission of collecting intelligence information and getting it back. Should the artillery not be adequately effective, then the next step would be calling in gunships or even air strikes from the Air Force. Calling your company commander for reinforcements is an additional option. The situation will develop from there. The problem solving methods will have developed into the decision making process. One just automatically leads into the other. That is a great deal of what leadership is all about. Here we also see where the bad and the ugly meet up with the good, the good being the further development of your leadership skills.

The benefits of the military experience never seem to stop, and I would say most of them are instrumental in dealing with stress. Next on this lengthy list is the learning and development of survival skills. Whether one remains in the military or transitions to civilian life, he or she can always feel confident, being able to survive under adverse conditions in a hostile environment, be it a war zone or on the streets of a major city. Sometimes there seem to be close similarities, particularly in today's world, which seems to get worse every day.

From the time a person enters the military, he is being trained in survival skills. Webster's dictionary defines the term survive as: to continue to exist, to outlast, and to outlive – in spite of hardship. We know that in basic training one is taught, among many other things, the skills of self-defense, individual weapons marksmanship, field-sanitation, basic communication skills, including hand and arm signals, and, of course, the physical training needed to build a body capable of dealing with the physical environment of a combat situation. Just about all of these areas tie directly into one's ability to survive under most conditions. Beyond basic training some of those same skills and many others are developed to an even greater degree. We must also consider that, if we do not develop the finest survival skills available anywhere, we might no longer expect to be the greatest military power in the world, the one that will outlast and outlive all others for all time. There you have it.

Another benefit of the military life I will mention is that of building a sense of humility. I can think of no major religion in this world of ours, certainly including Christianity, which does not identify an element of humility as an absolute necessity for reaching the ultimate peak of godliness if you like. Any Christian leader (or again any leader of any major religion) who does not possess that high quality of humility will not be an effective leader. It is a natural development in the military establishment. If we look to the dictionary once again, we find that being of a humble nature is being "modest and unassuming in attitude," as well as being respectful, and that would imply respect for all, regardless of rank or position.

The fact is, though it is an absolute requirement to show respect for a superior in the military, it is also necessary for a superior to show respect for his or her subordinates if he is to expect a genuine respect from the heart. A person who shows no genuine respect will never receive genuine respect. That is an absolute, and it is amazing how so many just do not seem to understand that incredibly simple concept. Along with the respect from subordinates comes a willingness to accomplish the mission. You will find that there is a great deal more cooperation and a building of the team spirit. People will want to work for you, rather than just feeling compelled to do so. There will be a significant difference in the overall performance of a unit under such conditions.

The other half of humility, modesty, is just as essential. There is little that is more irritating in my humble opinion than a military leader who is overbearing and obnoxious, and gives everyone the impression that he knows everything and there is no way that he could ever be wrong, nor will he ever admit to being wrong. In other words, he is trying his best to be super-human. It just doesn't work. Those who know what they are talking about do not have to try to prove to anyone that they know it. It becomes quite obvious to all by their actions. It is said that actions speak for themselves, as well as being "louder than words." Respect is earned by being humble and showing what you know by your actions, not by telling people how much you know.

Once again, a great example of a lesson learned in the area of humility comes to mind, and, though it does come from my life, it is one we all should heed. After being in Vietnam for somewhere between three and four months, still a second lieutenant, I transferred from the 196th L.I.B. up in the northern highlands down to the 199th L.I.B. in the Mekong Delta, south of Saigon. I had a rather tough time trying to convince everyone, including my superiors, that I was not just a brand new, green second lieutenant, fresh out of the States; that I had already had a bit of experience up north.

One of the first patrols with my new platoon was a night ambush. Shortly after departure from our base camp, we approached a small canal necessary to cross in order to continue on our route to the ambush site. After I had indicated that we were going across the canal, a few of the guys started to inflate air mattresses, preparing to load gear on them, which would involve taking a rope across to secure it to the other side, taking a half hour or more for the whole process. That sounded ludicrous to me. It was quite clear in my mind that all we had to do was raise our weapons and equipment over our heads and simply walk across the canal. It could not have been more than three and a half or four feet deep at most, and the whole thing would take five or ten minutes.

"Big Shot," who obviously knew it all, decided to lead by example. I raised my rifle over my head and proceeded to cross the canal. I just kept going, very confident with each step. I was knee-deep, waist-deep, chest-deep, helmet-deep and continuing to march. Finally, when the water level was quite far over my weapon, I began to evaluate what just happened. My feet were stuck firmly into the very soft mud beneath them, and I was having some serious thoughts about whether or not I could extract myself from this precarious position. I was unable to move at all. The mud was above my knees by this time.

Just before panic was ready to strike, I felt a pair of hands grab hold of my arms and weapon, and they pulled me free from the mud and into the bank to where I could climb out of the muck. I attempted to be very cool about the whole matter and merely said, "All right, let's blow up those air mattresses and get across this canal!" That was indeed an exercise in humility! I learned quickly to learn from those who know before jumping right into a situation about which I know little or nothing. I still had a great deal to learn. I truly believe that my men learned a great deal about me after I had made a bit of a fool of myself. It was quite apparent that I had learned my lesson and I became a very different person as a result of that incident. I only wish I could say that was the only exercise in humility I had to experience. Hey, we live and learn. That's a part of life.

I would be remiss if I were to leave the subject of humility without one additional great example of initiating an operation, having neglected one significant step in my planning. All who have attained any leadership position will be able to identify with this one. The AO (area of operations) was the same as the previous situation. I was new to the Mekong Delta, and

I was not at all familiar with the water patterns of that region, nor had I received any briefings on the subject. One of my first long-range missions was to take my platoon out about six to eight clicks (kilometers) from our company base camp, establish an all-night ambush site and return the next morning, usually a routine operation. I wanted to do everything perfectly, not only for the protection of my men, but because I needed to get off to a good start with my new unit and new commander. I really planned this whole operation in detail from the start. I even had the opportunity to do an aerial reconnaissance with a LOACH (OH-6 Cayuse), a light observation helicopter that looks like a bubble. I had already done a map recon and I knew exactly where I had to go, how to get there and how long it would take. The aerial recon was just to confirm that the real ground was what the map indicated it was. I had it all together and had calculated everything precisely.

In my planning, I took into account the three minor rivers that we had to cross to reach our site. I saw all three rivers on the map and I also located them on the ground from the helicopter. Each would take probably thirty to forty minutes to cross, since the rivers appeared to be small. The rest of the travel on foot would take a maximum of three hours to make, probably less. So, I allowed about two and a half hours for the river crossings and another three hours for the remainder of the trip. That was about five and a half hours. EENT (early evening nautical twilight, or dusk) was about 1930 hours (7:30 P.M.). By planning to leave five and a half hours before that time, it meant that our departure time would be about 1400 hours (2:00 P.M.). My platoon made last minute preparations for our operation, including having all of our equipment and weapons ready, and departed the base camp right on time. It seemed that there were no problems at all. We were ready to rock and roll!

Now, I can pass the buck with that previous comment that I was not properly briefed, and that does have some truth to it, but I was certainly guilty of not doing my homework properly, in that I was not aware that in the delta there is a phenomenon known as tidal changes. The delta is basically at sea level. As the ocean tides rise and fall, so does the water level in the entire delta. I never even considered the relationship between the ocean, which was quite far away, and the area in which I was working.

Between the time that I had taken my aerial recon and the time that my platoon departed on our mission, the tide had begun to rise. By the time we arrived at the vicinity of our ambush site, we had crossed not three minor rivers, but seven major rivers. The entire trip to the ambush site took us not five and a half hours, but close to ten hours! We were able to move into position approximately by midnight. That also meant that we had been in transit over four hours in total darkness, not entirely sure where we were at any given moment. It was almost miraculous that we even arrived where we were supposed to be, and I am still not entirely sure of that.

An additional good fortune was not running into any "hostiles" along the way. The trip to our ambush site was spooky in itself, and the rest of the night was not much different. I am also pleased to report that we never had to spring an ambush that night. We were probably not terribly alert after that rather exhausting trip. I am not certain today how that would have gone. Altogether, this whole ordeal was again a humbling experience, and I learned a great deal that day.

## CHAPTER 5 – TRANSITIONS

Probably one of the most significant elements of military life is that of making transitions from one walk of life into another and being able to have the flexibility to deal with the changes. The first one will be or will have been the initial transition from civilian life to the military establishment. Although requirements do have a tendency to change from time to time, as of the time of this writing the highest age for accepting people into the military is thirty-five years old. I can only imagine having lived in the civilian world for thirty-five years and then making the amazingly tough transition to military life. That would be as radical a change as my own family having undergone our move from coastal southern California to northern Michigan! Wow, both of those examples are going from one extreme to another. That would also mean that an individual of that age would have to remain on active duty until he or she was fifty-five years old to attain a fifty percent retirement, or sixty-one to attain a seventy-five percent retirement. Many people today are able to retire from the military before the age of forty. I can only speak for myself, being nearly seventy years old as I write, but I would definitely have a tough time keeping up with the eighteen- and nineteen-year-olds in the 82nd Airborne today. I did just that about thirty years ago and it was tough then. As a matter of fact, forget it. Today that would never happen. For some, perhaps, it could happen, but I would not bet on it. I learned a great deal about the physical conditioning of the 82nd Airborne with a mere three-week tour of duty with them. I acquired even more respect for them after my short tour than I had had before, which was a great deal.

In Chapter One, in reference to training, I covered many of the transitional elements one makes in military life. However, there is a great deal more that should be considered. The impact of every transition is going to differ remarkably between any two individuals. It is going to vary, depending upon background, current lifestyle, attitudes, aspirations and anything else that makes a person who he or she is.

The initial transition from civilian to military life can be quite natural and very easy, or it can be a borderline traumatic experience. Let's say you were born with the proverbial silver spoon in your mouth, and your parents were part of the upper crust or among the jet setters, and they decided to send you off to a military school to complete your education through high school.

That could mean that your parents did not really have time for raising you themselves. Your attitude could very well determine how you would be able to deal with the transition to full-time military. Number one, you might have a very negative feeling about the military in general. That being the case, the decision for the military, you would later find out, would have been a bad choice. On the other hand, if your experiences with the military school had been very positive and you excelled in everything and enjoyed it, then you would have made an excellent decision and would probably enjoy the vast majority of it. You would be very well prepared for that life style.

For an individual who had been associated with gang life on the streets of New York City, Los Angeles, Detroit or Chicago, the transition could have had far different impact. That person would have been from a situation where he would have to have made it on his own, and then perhaps relied upon the wrong types of people for support and perhaps even relied on drugs for his survival in that culture. His transition to military life will really be a challenge. He will have many more obstacles to confront than the majority of his peers. He will be among the types of people with whom he probably has never had to deal before. To be successful he will have to change more than most people, who have not come from such a background. Yet, he could turn out to be the best of the best in his efforts to remain on top, and he will probably have the strong desire that it takes, if for no other reason, than he sees the possibility for success. Besides that, he will be quite accustomed to dealing with major obstacles in life. Survival skills would be among his strongest assets.

This major transition will also encompass the quality of self-discipline. Can the individual accept the regimented style of the military? Suddenly he is required to "rise and shine" each and every day at the crack of dawn, go through all the morning rituals, not at his own pace, but at that of an obnoxious drill sergeant hammering at him every moment of every hour of every day. He is expected to fully cooperate without question and continue to get on with his life, even if it does not even seem like his life. Guess what? It is a whole new life! He either has to accept it or reject it and many choose the latter. They just cannot do it.

Once that initial transition is made, the rest is pretty much a "piece of cake." Life goes on quite smoothly and everything begins to be very normal. It is no different today than it was nearly fifty years ago when I did it. I have had two sons in the Army, and I have seen them go through the same routines that I went through way back in the sixties. They have taken different directions, but the processes have not been remarkably different. They both were deployed one or more times in the Middle East, and both did extremely well after those experiences. Both of them have had different directions with regard to their interests, and have gone different directions upon leaving the military. Neither decided to make it a full-time career, but one never knows what might happen to change the course of events in their lives or in the world for that matter.

My eldest son would never have even considered military service, as he has never had the type of personality conducive to that life. He has plans that go far into the future as a geologist who studies volcanoes and lava flows. He has attained his master's degree and has done a great deal of work towards his PhD. He too will be living his life on the edge, but in an entirely different way. Your attitudes and intentions in life might be oriented in one direction now, but you just never know what the future may present. Circumstances prevail and sometimes control our decisions and our futures.

There is a vast array of additional transitions that one goes through during his or her career in the military, regardless of how long that service may be. One significant group of transitions to address should be promotions. Each time one of those occurs, the person, by the nature of the promotion itself, must undergo some changes. Each promotion requires the individual to accept, not only a larger paycheck, but also a greater amount of responsibility. This process is not unlike much of civilian life, but the ramifications are usually much greater. As previously mentioned, growth begins to occur, mentally and psychologically. As that growth continues, frequently new values emerge, new perspectives develop, new attitudes and concepts come to the surface, and, before that person realizes it, he has become a whole new individual, hopefully for the better. He might see not only his own life differently, but the entire world from a completely different point of view than he did a year or two earlier. A full, life-long career may never have entered his mind, particularly during his early years in the military, but considering the fact that things change rather remarkably after all the training, some of which may have been unpleasant, and the negatives are long past, the big picture could well look much more appealing.

Other transitions would of course be in relocating to parts of the world you might never have thought you would ever visit, let alone live for lengthy periods of time. They might include places that many view as exotic, places that may well seem like another planet, places that you feel are worse than you would imagine hell to be, or places that seem entirely too nice for American military presence. I have been in the heat of battle many times in Vietnam, and I have been in what one might call the lap of luxury at the Presidio of San Francisco, California. Each assignment gives you a different view and perspective of life. Each new area provides a different group of people to whom you are exposed, and each is an education in itself, allowing you to see for yourself how others live and think.

There are not only the new areas in which to work, but there are also opportunities to travel while on assignment. The continent upon which you are working might well determine how far your travels might take you. All of these foreign experiences will continue to broaden your horizons and educate you further in your views of the world. To remain flexible and open to new ideas and ways of life is the real key to success and individual growth.

One example of my own further education to the world through travel is a trip to Panama many years ago. In my younger days I had a rather limited knowledge of the world, except for what I had learned in high school and college classes, looking at maps and learning bits of history here and there. I had no clue what to expect when I learned that I would be going to Panama for a couple of weeks. It was just another Latin American country as far as I knew.

My natural presumption was that the inhabitants of Panama were brown-skinned, Hispanic-looking people who spoke Spanish. The big surprise was when I looked around and noticed that almost all those Spanish-speaking people were black. I had never been in an area where I was surrounded by black people all speaking Spanish. I thought that was pretty awesome; certainly unique for me and a real eye-opener. It occurred to me how limited my views of the rest of the world were. Only when I visited England, even though I had heard many times over that England and America were "two countries divided by a common language," did it occur to me just how true that statement was. I was there for about six weeks, and it took me at least two weeks just to figure out what anybody was saying. In the vicinity of Aldershot, not far out of London, it was like listening to a foreign language. I suppose it is not a great deal different than most Americans visiting the bayou country of Louisiana, which could be a whole new cultural experience in itself.

With regard to transitions, I can't help but think about the really significant differences between where you are physically and emotionally when on active duty in the military and what you observe on the "outside" in the civilian world. You may well not be old enough to have lived through the '50s and '60s, but you certainly must be aware that it was a very special time in many ways, much different from what we see today. It was the "cold war" era.

For most it was a serious time when sirens went off every day at noon as tests for early warning of a nuclear attack, when, at least once a week, the schools went through drop drills for an eventual nuclear attack, which we were all sure would really happen one day, and tension was extremely high.

Our transitions of times were just as significant as transitions of place. The situations changed radically, as did the psychological impact. Feelings for the military were considerably different too. We were not nearly as concerned about the soldier on the ground back then as we were for our own survival of a nuclear holocaust. America had missiles and total annihilation on our minds, rather than the individual soldier who might never even be a major part of the big picture.

A few years later, still in the '60's, we also had the infamous hippie movement all over the country, and I happened to be stationed at the Presidio of San Francisco, California for about a year and a half in 1968 and 1969. Every morning on my way to work and on my way home in the evening I passed through Haight Ashbury, one of the biggest hippie colonies in California. We all know how the hippies felt about the military and the war in Vietnam; it was basically, "Make love, not war." They just stared at me driving by and I smiled and waved at them and gave them my thumbs up. This was after I had returned from Vietnam, and I did not have overly positive feelings for them either. I really felt that I would love to have had some of them over in that country, along with me and the other half million or so American troops there at the time.

Depending on how much active duty a person serves, he or she may decide or perhaps have obligations to do some time in the reserve components, as both of my sons, Brent and Scott, did after discharge from active duty. Every branch of service has reserve forces, and, of course, each individual state has its own Army National Guard, and some have Air National Guard organizations. If a person elects to come off active duty, he or she may or may not have specific obligations, but they will always have the option to continue with the military through any of those reserve component organizations. That way they can go off into civilian life again, and at the same time remain affiliated with the military. Those are the folks we refer to as "citizen soldiers." I was in that category for a very long time.

Sometimes the military just gets into your blood and it is difficult to say good-bye to it. Not only that, but you can actually have a second career going for you that can develop into a second retirement after at least twenty years total. Your active duty time combines with reserve time to add up to a retirement. The only difference between retiring from active duty and retiring from the reserve components is that from active duty, retirement compensation comes right away. Retirement from the reserves will bring retirement compensation only after age 60, and the monthly total will be somewhat less after retirement from the reserve components. Trust me; it is still nice with that monthly check coming in without interruption. It is a very reliable, steady, extra income.

There are several changes that one must get used to when transitioning to civilian life. Whether it is active duty or reserve components, the element of travel always comes into play. Even though the Army only gave me retirement credit for a bit over twenty-two years (they can only give credit for good years, those being years during which you receive 50s retirement points either for academics or for drill days), I actually served for over thirty years. During those thirty years I had so many opportunities to travel that it more than made everything worthwhile. Per usual, there was always the continuing good, bad and ugly, but honestly the majority was very good. That's what makes that life so interesting. "Variety is the spice of life." I have been to Europe, Asia, Central America, Australia and, of course, numerous areas of the US, to include Alaska and Hawaii. I loved just having been able to see so much of the world.

For most people who are in the reserve components, the majority of travel time is during the summer months, but there are many units that have to travel to their drill sites for that one weekend out of each month. My California Army National Guard unit, which was an armor battalion, had to travel out to the desert each month for training and maintenance on the tanks. We would leave on a Friday night and come back Sunday afternoon, which did not interfere at all with my job as a high school teacher. Now and then I would have to leave for a couple of weeks during the academic year for other training or military exercises, and that would make things a little awkward, but most employers have been understanding, and things generally work out pretty well. Most of them tend to be at least tolerant, but if not, they are also required by law to give necessary time to military matters and let their people off work for those purposes. Some employers have a tough time of it when their employees are deployed over-seas for lengthy periods of time. Our government requires that all employers must offer those employees their jobs back upon return from deployment. That never happened to me, but it does happen often these days, as many can attest to. Some have had to fight for some of their rights.

When a person belongs to an active reserve unit, he or she is required to work one weekend per month, and two weeks of continuous duty at some point during the year, usually, as previously indicated, during the summer. Again, that duty could be done locally or it could involve travel to a distant location. Much depends upon the type of unit to which one belongs. If it is a combat arms unit, and it is located in an urban environment, then more than likely the unit will need to go to another location than their home armory for unit training. They would need a location that would be conducive or appropriate for unit tactical training, whether it is straight-leg infantry on the ground or with tactical vehicles, both wheeled and tracked. It could also involve aircraft or heavy equipment.

Most people in active military units give those in reserve components a rough time, and there is always a bit of rivalry between the two. A good example of that is when you hear an active duty person tell another, "It is 1400 hours, 2:00 P.M. national guard time." Just as with inter-service rivalry, it is usually a healthy rivalry, but the origins of some of those seeming hostilities are not always well founded. Frequently people in the active components consider the reserve units to be untrained and not prepared to go into a combat environment successfully. They often make a false presumption that because the active components train nearly every day, and the reserve units can only train about forty days per year the reserve units cannot possibly be capable of being anywhere near the active unit's levels of training.

I can attest to the fact that there are many reserve units that are at excellent levels of training and could very well compete with some of their comparable active units, and might well be even better prepared to accomplish their assigned missions. On the other hand, there are certainly those that have a long way to go before being prepared to go into combat. There are frequently some very good and justifiable reasons for their not being prepared, and, more often than not, they have to go through a tremendous amount of training upon receiving orders for deployment before the units are actually deployed. The units are evaluated each year and given a readiness level. If they are not at the required level of readiness, then they are given a certain amount of time to reach that level, and are expected to meet those goals on time.

With regard to assessing the effectiveness of a reserve component unit I again have an appropriate example. I spent the majority of my military career in the US Army Reserve, but, as I've stated, I did give a couple of years to the California Army National Guard. During that time I was the company commander of a tank company in Escondido, California. That was, indeed, a very nice assignment and I enjoyed nearly every part of it, even though I had little training behind me in the armor branch and with tanks. I had great fun with the unit and enjoyed going out to the desert for training. I had the opportunity to personally drive the M-48A1 tank and fire the 50 caliber machine guns, as well as the main gun. As Mel Brooks might say, "It's good to be king" (or commander in this case). Most of that was truly exhilarating and I have no regrets. However, there was one element that I came to dislike about my position as company commander, and that was the requirement for recruitment. I thought that I was quite good at it, but my way of recruiting differed a great deal from that of my superiors. You can see again how some of these good and bad things can tend to overlap. Here is one of those subordinate/superior relationships again.

Once again, in my ever-so-humble opinion, the only way to build the very best unit is to find the very best people for the jobs. Unfortunately, the opinions of my superiors had nothing to do with quality. The only requirement they emphasized was quantity. Their ideas were probably that anyone could be trained. Granted, they were undoubtedly being pressured from above to get their numbers up, as recruitment had been on the decline in the early '70s, both in the active and reserve components. I had not been meeting the required numbers to meet my quota, but I was really progressing nicely in building a unit with some quality people, those who were excited about being in the unit, had some intelligence, and showed great potential for leadership. In addition, they were closely tied to the community. I felt very good about that.

I finally went "head to head" with my battalion commander, and he let me know in no uncertain terms that he did not care about what kind of people I recruited into my unit, as long as the numbers came up to quota. I let him know that I was not willing to take the "ash and trash" off the streets just to bring his precious numbers up. I was aiming for quality and would not accept anything less. If he insisted on anything other than that, he could give my job to someone else. Well, guess what? That marked the end of my California National Guard career. I returned to the Army Reserve. I would not want to imply that all National Guard units are like that. That was a given time in a given place with special circumstances, and that was my own experience. I would hope that it is not like that today. Then again, one must always be prepared for anything. Flexibility is critical, but not to the extent of defeating the whole purpose of improving the quality, effectiveness and professionalism of military units.

The flip side of that coin can well illustrate the first point I was making with regard to reserve components being at a very high state of readiness. In the beginning of my command of the tank company, and up to the point of the confrontation regarding recruitment techniques, that unit was as prepared for deployment as one could ever expect, given the amount of time we could put into training, and vehicle and other equipment maintenance requirements. Even though our personnel strength was lower than it should have been, we, as a unit, accomplished more during our weekend drills and two weeks per year of annual training than most active component units working all year around and full-time. My men were amazing, and nearly all the soldiers of that unit had the right attitudes to get the job done and do it well. I was more than just a little proud of my unit's accomplishments, and I do not take the credit for that.

As well as the main mission of a reserve or national guard unit, the unit has additional responsibilities, with, of course, much less time to accomplish them than active units. Because the members are "citizen soldiers," they live within the confines of a city or town, and have added responsibilities to the community in which they live. Their armories are often used for the purposes of community activities, and some of those activities are actually sponsored by and manned by the soldiers of that unit. Frequently the time necessary for these activities is donated by the individuals within the unit, just because they feel the responsibility as members of that community, and because they take pride in people coming to that facility for those activities. It gives them more exposure to the people of that community. It is in fact their facility and the people are almost part of their family and, therefore, there is a strong connection and a personal pride that is difficult to describe, but always present.

This symbiotic relationship encompasses a feeling that most members of an active unit would probably never be able to understand unless they were to experience it. The community and the military unit actually bond to a degree if the activities are successful. There is a common respect, and, when that happens, that is when a community is deeply affected and emotionally moved when a unit is deployed in times of war. If a member of that unit is lost as a casualty of war, it is a personal loss to the whole town, rather than just the unit and the family of that person. As I implied, the community actually becomes like an extended family.

Being in the reserve components is one avenue you might take after coming off active duty. The other direction would, of course, lead you directly into the civilian work force, not being a part of any military structure. If you do not have the ability or means to seek employment while on active duty, the military will often help you find a compatible work place out in the "real world." After having spent three to five years on active duty, however, you may well not find it the easiest thing you've ever done to make your transition back into your previous life. You may find that that life does not even exist anymore. Today, of course, there are also social networks on line that have past and current military people more than willing to assist in the transition process.

As much as I sometimes do not care to admit it, I have become very much a part of today's world of technology, even though I have not mastered many of the techniques to improve my proficiency. In other words, I am a bit lame when it comes to that. On the other hand, I have discovered a good deal about social networking. One avenue that ties directly into military people transitioning back to the civilian world is with the LinkedIn network. There are several groups that welcome people coming off from active duty, not only in finding a new job in the new life they are beginning, but being there to assist in coming back to a world that has long forgotten them.

In the LinkedIn network, as well as many others, there are groups very specific to the person's military experience. There are many that have had nearly identical experiences, who are more than willing to give advice to anyone seeking it. There are professionals on line who make it a business to help military veterans come back into civilian society and be successful. The help is there for the taking and does not cost a dime. I try to be there as often as possible myself, just because I went through some of it myself many years ago, and I feel that I can give some pretty good advice sometimes. It is generally very much appreciated by those who seek it.

A great deal can change dramatically over the period of time you will have been on active duty. You will find that your old friends have either left town to start a new life, gone off to college or trade school, have traveled off somewhere to find themselves, and there will be at least one or two behind bars at the county jail or state prison. Some will undoubtedly still be in town, but have entirely different life styles than you remember. Some may well have begun families of their own, and, therefore, do not have the ability or desire to go off doing whatever you remember them doing with you in the "good old days."

My youngest son, Scott, can be a great example to illustrate here, whether or not he may appreciate it. After having been in the Army for four years, as an Army Ranger, Scott was twenty-three years old, coming off active duty. He went to Michigan Technical University to attain his degree in forestry to begin a whole new career. Upon graduation with a bachelor's degree in hand, he went to work with the Department of Natural Resources (DNR) in the state of Washington, working in the Pacific Cascade region. He absolutely loved the work, but his desire was to be hired on with the US Forest Service, hopefully to return to Michigan.

Scott is an outdoorsy kind of guy. He loves it and is great at what he does. As you can see, he is a young man with a specific goal, and an extremely strong desire to fulfill all of it. He was assisted in the cost of his continuing education with the help of his GI Bill benefits, and he did extremely well at a school that had very high academic expectations. He was also a member of the Army Reserve, which was augmenting his income and the cost of going to school. That did become inconvenient for him, however, just because there was not a reserve unit near him with his school being in the far northern reaches of the upper peninsula of Michigan.

Let's throw him back in the present tense for a moment. Coming home for visits, he finds many of his old friends and acquaintances are not even in his old hometown anymore. Of the ones that are left, he finds some, not necessarily his closest friends, have been in and out of jail. Since this town happens to be one of those where many go almost right from high school into trouble and off to jail, some are still doing the same things that he used to do in high school. This includes things like guzzling beer and playing Nintendo or other stupid video games. Some have not matured or developed at all intellectually, in their array of experiences, or in any other way, with the exception of adding several inches around their waists. Some are not only clueless as to what they want to do with their lives, but have not so much as given it any thought since high school. How much does Scott have in common with these people? I'm not saying he is no longer sociable or does not like to down a few beers with his closest friends, but he is not really the same Scott who left this town many years ago. And, yes, there were also some who actually did move into directions that had a future, but unfortunately very few.

Having gone off to college, Scott found himself in a rather foreign environment. He found that he was not only five years out of the average freshman age category, but he had different attitudes and ideas about nearly everything. He had already experienced much more of the world than the vast majority of his peers perhaps ever would. He found some who had been through similar experiences to his own, and they shared some common interests. Scott showed that it is good for those who are off to college by themselves to have at least one friend with whom to share things important and that the two might have in common. When you are at an institution of higher learning and far away from home, you really do need to find others who share some of your own ideas and attitudes. Scott did that, and it worked very well for him. As a side note, while I am finishing up the last minute changes to this book, Scott and his family are headed to that job he wanted so badly with the US Forest Service, as it was offered to him a short time ago. Everything worked out wonderfully for him. He is one happy veteran.

There are probably hundreds of things that people leaving the military would never think about with regard to making a transition back to civilian life. There are hundreds of thousands of young people coming off of active duty and back into the potentially "cold, cruel world." It certainly can be that way, but does not have to be. Good direction, setting specific goals, anticipating the potential obstacles, and knowing in advance how to successfully deal with those obstacles are at least some of the keys to success on the outside. Going completely blindly into that change in lifestyles could very well be disastrous, and certainly has been for many.

Let's also be perfectly honest and up front about those who have gone through traumatic war experiences and have been affected to the extent of having symptoms of P.T.S.D. (post-traumatic stress disorder). If they have not gone through proper psychological counseling and therapy, there is a more than good chance that they will have difficulty dealing with just about every aspect of civilian life. They will have almost no ability to set goals for themselves, and they will be disoriented in life and unable to adjust to anything. It is usually these people who go to drugs, alcohol or any other addictive habits. These are the ones who absolutely have to seek help, and the VA is always the best place to start. I understand that recently in some areas the VA has not always been available for everyone. They are being pushed way beyond their current capacities. It was not anticipated by our government that we would have anything near the needs that exist today from our returning troops; those coming back to civilian life. VA has become overwhelmed today.

There is definitely help out there for everyone, but all need to be resourceful to find it. It really does become easier every day with the astronomically growing Internet. You can find anything that the human mind can conceive of these days, and that includes all kinds of support, employment opportunities, and even new or old friends. There are no longer any limits and no valid excuses for being unable to find sources for any kind of help. Transitioning to civilian life has naturally become easier than it has ever been before, at least in that respect.

A transition of the family from military life to the civilian world can also be very significant. If your family has been accustomed to living on a military installation with all of the conveniences right within reach, to include family housing, which is provided at no cost, nearby schools, the commissary and exchange facilities, tax-free, and all of the other businesses that are associated with the exchange, then all of their habits will have to change. They will have to adapt to whatever changes are within the new community in which they live. They will miss the convenience of having everything located within the same square mile or so, as it normally is on a military facility. Dad will have to find a new barbershop, mom will have to find a new beauty salon and the children will be attending a new school with a considerably different group of kids than they have been used to.

Nearly everything will be much more expensive than most of you have been used to. In order for the family to survive well financially, both mom and dad will have to have higher incomes than before, and the kids will probably expect a higher allowance than they might have had before. Without a good deal of prior planning, the family could very well have to reevaluate their whole life style. That is why, in making the decision to change from military to civilian life, the military person better have a good, solid, stable job to move into. There will be so many extra things that pop up unexpectedly that it is very difficult to enumerate all of them here. Medical insurance is, of course, another major consideration, as the family will have been used to everything being provided by the military; all of their medical and dental coverage has been provided, and dad's or mom's new job better provide all of that, or the family may be up for a rather rude awakening.

My middle son, Brent, came off from active duty and thought that everything would be pretty simple. He had married a young lady six months or so before separating from the Army. Aside from their two ferrets and two dogs, it seemed like it would be smooth sailing into a new life in the civilian world. He was stationed at Fort Bragg, North Carolina, and was pretty much guaranteed a nice job as a mechanic at a new car dealership in Daytona Beach, Florida. They found a very nice place to rent, quite close to work, and it seemed like everything was good to go. They made their move on time, and, when they were all settled in, Brent discovered that he had been put on hold with the dealership and his job. They were not quite ready to put him to work, as they had agreed. Things happen, right?

Although Brent could have fallen back on unemployment, as he was eligible for it after coming off from active duty, he chose not to. His job was just on hold for a while. He and his new wife had not been opposed to spending a good deal of money, and living the best life they could afford, and that included hitting the gambling casinos now and then, which they enjoyed very much. They had also gone quite a bit into debt. They had bills to pay and no income; not a great combination. He had to start looking for other work as it became more apparent that his promised job might never materialize.

He connected with an organization that wanted to make him a vehicle retriever driver over in Iraq. Oh, that sounded great, after his having already been to Afghanistan for a year with the Army. The good news was that they would pay him $92,000 per year, tax-free. The bad news was that the job was in Iraq. He was seriously considering it. He and his wife had made their final decision to do it when it suddenly occurred to them that the company was going to require him to go to truck-driving school, the cost of which would come out of his pocket, at the tune of about $8,000 on the spot. That would take about three weeks, plus there was another two weeks of training in Texas. In addition to the cost of the driving school, he would have zero income for five weeks. Well, that was too much to expect. That plan was dead. Do you see where we are going with this? The saga is not yet over. He thought he had carefully considered everything, and things went wrong.

If you, with or without a family, were ever forced to make a transition from civilian life into the military, you more than likely thought that it was a pretty rough proposition. However, going the other way around can, without a doubt, be even tougher. The military establishment, contrary to what many believe, really does tend to "take care of its own." In a way, you have a whole community surrounding you with never-ending protection. You have neighbors all around you in very similar situations who can offer not only empathy, but also expertise and good advice regarding whatever problems you may encounter. They can and most often do pitch in and help others through those problems.

Unit commanders can find help for their people and their families as soon as the problem is identified. It may sound like there are some strong similarities between this and what was previously discussed with the National Guard and the surrounding community, but the active military develops a much stronger community, all of whom have nearly everything in common. Did Brent find that kind of help in Daytona Beach? I don't think so. Was it a wise move on Brent's part to leave the Army? It seemed so at the time, and I'm quite sure it will prove to be as time goes on. The fact was that Brent had no desire to remain in the Army. Things have a tendency to work out for the best, and the Army did not seem to be where his heart was. He came back from his military experiences a much better man, and his acquired skills are paying off nicely today.

There is an additional development that came up a couple of years ago with Brent's deployment to Afghanistan. While his unit was deployed, the families of all of the soldiers of his unit formed a support group for their men and women. They made up care packages for them, wrote letters, had a welcoming committee for their return, and did as much as humanly possible for the troops while they were away from home. How many employers in the civilian world would even care enough to offer help to their employees? While there are exceptions in the civilian world, you are on your own; it is either sink or swim, and generally, no one will be out there to throw you the proverbial life preserver unless it is family or extraordinary friends.

Previously we discussed training situations on bases within the United States, but after training is all over and the individual is assigned to a permanent unit, life is significantly different. No longer are you in a barracks with fifty or sixty people on the same bay. You now are normally living in a room with a private bath, probably sharing that room with one other person. It offers much more privacy and you no longer have a drill sergeant breathing down your neck every minute. All units are not the same. Some will have much nicer accommodations than others, and some installations are just newer and nicer than others. Life in general will have changed remarkably for the better, and, as life goes on, it will more than likely continue to improve. You are treated much more like a real live human being, and even the job that you will have will be more like a civilian job, except that everyone seems to wear the same attire. Maybe that's why they call it a uniform. Ya think?

Frequently people think about the military in terms of its men and women being stationed on an installation out in the middle of nowhere, as indeed some are, but that is by no means always the case. Very often military installations are right in the middle of a major metropolis. The Navy is notorious for that. Most major naval bases are located in large cities, such as San Diego and San Francisco in California, and Virginia Beach, Norfolk and Chesapeake in Virginia. Life in those areas can be eye-openers if you are not used to the "big city" atmosphere. A great deal depends on your upbringing. If you were brought up in a metropolitan area and find yourself at an installation near a very small town, then you must make a transition to two very different environments; one being the installation itself and the other being the small town next to the military installation. The exact opposite also applies for the individual from a small town going to a post in a metropolitan area.

One must always be extremely flexible if he or she expects to be successful with the military life. Prepare for the unexpected and adapt to it, because it is inevitable. More than likely, you will actually learn to enjoy it. Notice how many retired military people settle in the same town from which they retired. Some find it nearly impossible to make a complete break from the military establishment. They still want to be in close proximity, even if they are no longer playing an active role. They enjoy continuing to see people in uniform. They still have many friends on active duty, as well as those who have previously retired and remained in the area.

Many of those people, after coming off active duty and remaining in the same town as the installation, particularly after a retirement, elect to go back to work as civilians, perhaps even in the same capacity as they were in the military. Many years ago, before several changes were made, there were many who accomplished what was called "double dipping." They would stay in the military long enough to acquire the highest possible retirement, and then begin a new civilian career with the military as a civil servant. If they retired at the rank of lieutenant colonel or full colonel, they could well begin a new job as a GS 10 or 12, which would be a very high paying position, and after another twenty years attain a second healthy retirement. I ran into a few of those people when I was assigned at Sixth Army Headquarters at the Presidio of San Francisco. It was a nicely kept little secret for a long time until Uncle Sam finally discovered the problem and put the brakes on it, and it is not done anymore.

After a military career, however, civil service is still certainly another option and a very viable and lucrative career choice. After twenty or more years of military experience you have what it takes to make a very successful civil service employee. You may well have already been trained for the position before you start. For many the only change is in clothing. As a civilian, of course, you would not have any obligations of overseas assignments, although that would still be an option. You would have a permanent position as long as you were able or as long as the installation remained active. Recently, however, there have been many installations inactivated by the federal government. If you worked for one of those installations, you would go the way of the installation; you would probably be history. Then again there are chances for reassignment, depending upon one's flexibility for relocation.

Those are the risks however. It is not all that different than civilian life. If you are working for a company that goes "belly-up," then you would also be part of where that company goes; out on the street. Life is never certain, regardless of what direction you take. Get used to it. If one were to compare the stability of the military as opposed to most civilian companies, who do you think would win out? Chances of the military going "belly-up" are fairly slim I should think. Then again, nothing is impossible!

While on the subject of civilians working for the military, I, among many others, had some significant difficulties with a few of them, and that has given me just a bit of an attitude with regard to that group of people. While I would by no means attempt to categorize them into one contiguous group with common thoughts and actions, I have noticed a certain commonality with those who seemed to have worked in their positions a bit too long. Many seemed to think that they were in charge of everything and everyone. Granted, some had been high-ranking officers while they were on active duty, but that still did not give them more authority than their position entailed.

As a general truism, which most in the military accept, civilians out-rank military, but that is not to say that any of those civilians should have the authority to degrade military people and treat them as sub-humans. Unfortunately, that is exactly what happens within the military establishment. Sometimes even rather low-ranking civilians are given a little authority and it goes straight to their heads, and they tend to act like they are some kind of royalty. They frequently act like they are installation commanders or commanding generals, except that they are often not as nice.

Both before and way beyond the end of my active duty in the US Army I had opportunities to work with many civilians within the Army community, many of whom were absolutely wonderful people, very effective in their jobs, and they were great with the military people with whom they worked. Many of those with whom I worked were at the Presidio, and some I worked with while I was with the reserve components. None of those people did I ever have a complaint about.

Many years after my active duty, after having been in the reserve components for several years, I had some problems with receiving academic credit for a large portion of the Army Infantry Career Course that I had successfully completed. The logical recourse was to call the Infantry School, located at Fort Benning, Georgia.

Upon calling the Infantry School, I spoke to the lady who claimed to be in charge of academic records. I asked her why I was not receiving credit for two of the four phases of the course that I had completed. She informed me, after having checked my records, that I had taken the "older curriculum course work" and that I had to do the work again with the revised edition. I told her that the phases I had completed were the phases that her office had sent to me. I had no way of knowing that they were out of date. She could not have cared less about any of that. The fact was that I had not completed what was then current. After a good deal of arguing with a "brick wall," I weakened and submitted to her, and told her to send all the new coursework to me, and I would do it all again.

I received that work and completed it again in the designated time. Once again, I did not receive credit for it. Again, I called and inquired as to the reason for again not receiving credit for the work. She had no record of my having submitted the work. I had acquired the habit of documenting everything by this time in my career. I told her that I had all the documentation I needed for proof. She had no intention of even listening to me or any of my arguments. She, knowing that she was right and I was wrong, just cut me off, and that was to be the end of it.

Well, she obviously did not know me very well, or she would never have attempted that nonsense. I had no intention of even trying to deal with that office again. I contacted my local congressman, explained the whole situation and turned it over to him to straighten out. It took nearly two years, but without that coursework behind me, I was not eligible for promotion. After all was said and done, I had credit for the work completed (twice) and it was all worked out, and I was later promoted without a hitch, but not without help "from above." The promotion was also retroactive, which also meant that I had more money coming to me.

Many years later and after many years of dealing with similar people as the lady mentioned above, I was informed that my time for mandatory retirement had arrived. I had received a form that basically inquired as to whether or not I wished to be transferred to retirement status or just discharged. That in essence meant that I would either accept my retirement or donate it to the US government. At the time, I thought it was one of the stupidest inquiries I had ever seen, but it was an absolute requirement to complete the form and submit it in order to receive retirement benefits. There is no way in the world I would ever not have responded to that request. It was a good part of my future. I mean, that was an absolute "no-brainer," right? Wrong.

Several months later, I received discharge papers! The reason I followed the previous statement with an exclamation point is that, if you are not familiar with the system, a discharge is much different from being transferred into retirement. Being transferred into retirement means that you are still an active part of the military; you are merely in retirement status, and will at the age of sixty receive retirement pay each month. If you are discharged, you are no longer a part of anything unless you still have a continuing commitment. After a discharge all of your paperwork merely disappears into the ether. Your file gets shipped off to the archives, which means that, for all practical purposes, you no longer exist! That is what happened to me.

As needless as it might be to say, I was not at all a "happy camper." As soon as I received my discharge, I was on the phone making inquiries. Of course, per usual, I connected with a wonderful, civilian with whom I had a delightful, meaningful conversation. It began with my asking why I might have been discharged, as opposed to being transferred into retirement status. Well, she assured me that I should have been sent a form on which to decide whether I wanted a discharge or transfer to retirement, and I apparently made my decision for discharge. I naturally responded with something like, "Are you kidding me or what? Would anyone honestly think that I would work for thirty years toward retirement and suddenly decide that the US government has been so wonderful to me that I want to, out of the kindness of my heart, donate my retirement back to that government? I may have something of a giving heart, but that kind of a philanthropist I cannot afford to be."

Well, to make a long story somewhat shorter, she told me how sorry she was, but I had made my decision and there was nothing she could do about it now. That did not set well with me. "Wrong answer!" I told her. I responded that I did not recall ever receiving that notice, and, if I had received it, I certainly would not have responded in a way that would have killed a perfectly good career. That would not have made any sense whatsoever. She refused to listen to my plea. There was simply nothing she could or would do about it. Before ending our conversation, I told her, "Ma'am, before you hang up, I want to be perfectly clear about one thing; you have not heard the last of this. I have already initiated and won my case with one congressional investigation, and I am not in the slightest way disinclined to initiate another one, and I will win again! Do you understand what I am saying?" At that point she hung up on me.

I will again attempt to be brief. It all caught up to them again, right in the old posterior. This time it was a congressional/senatorial investigation, and, although it took nearly two years to complete, Lieutenant Colonel McClarren ended up in retirement where he belonged. Why, I still ask today, was all of that nonsense necessary? It was necessary merely because one, lone civil service employee, commonly referred to as "civil serpents" for good reason, had decided that she was powerful enough to kill the career of a patriotic soldier and combat veteran, with thirty years of service behind him, and have no remorse whatsoever about it.

I apologize if I seem to have tooted my own horn a bit, but it was very disturbing at the time and remains so today. If you happen to be a civil service employee, I certainly want to emphasize that those kinds of people exist in every walk of life, and I am among the first to acknowledge that, but there have been several instances that have tended to leave me with a rather negative attitude about such people working for the military. I leave it at that. My advice, of course, is that not only should all of us have flexibility, but also the determination to be ready to fight for what has been earned and deserved. Let no one stand in the way of your rights, no matter what.

## Chapter 6 – Women In The Military

The role of women in the military has changed remarkably over the last sixty or seventy years, and for the benefit of my young, female readers, there has never been a better time than right now for women in the military. Opportunities for developing a truly rewarding career are abundant, and things are getting better all the time. During the Second World War, each branch of the service had its own contingency of women in the military workforce. We had the WACS, the WAMS and the WAVES (Army, Marines and Navy). It was only later that men and women all became part of the whole, and discrimination between the sexes for the most part disappeared, although that aspect may remain arguable.

Women have been given expanded responsibilities and occupational specialties, which, until recently, did not include the combat arms, of which infantry is one. The fact is, in the past, we, as an American fighting force, have not figured out how the sexes can be mixed effectively in a combat environment. There are just too many issues that develop that can and do interfere with combat effectiveness. We sometimes discuss the humorous parts of men and women sharing a foxhole or just having to go to the bathroom, the facilities of which are nonexistent in the field. Sexuality issues in the military have come more to the forefront over the last twenty years than ever before. Now we have accepted women in the infantry, both in the Marines and the Army. There are few, if any restrictions now on what occupations women can assume in any of the military services. As I write, the Army and Marines are still trying to evaluate the effectiveness of the most recent changes in their structure with regard to women in the combat arms.

There is no doubt that women have greater opportunity for advancement today than they ever had in the past. It was not long ago that a woman could reach the rank of O-6 (a captain in the Navy or Coast Guard, or a colonel in the Army, Marines or Air Force), but no further. Today we have women as generals or flag officers in most of the services, now even as high as four-star general. None can argue that sexual discrimination in the military should be allowed when it comes to levels of intelligence or the decision making process.

As it currently stands, with women only beginning to become active in the combat arms, it would make little sense to place a woman in command of a combat unit. We will not find a woman as an infantry division commander any time soon, just because of a lack of experience in that field. However, a female commanding general of any other branch would no longer be unusual. The Army has allowed women in staff positions of combat arms for some time now, but only at division or higher levels of command. The policy is currently still in the process of change.

Over the last few years we have seen the first female commandant of the Army's Drill Instructor School, who was a command sergeant major, and we have seen women reach the highest rank possible, that of four-star general. We have in essence seen unwritten rules and traditions broken by the tearing down of sexual discrimination. There is currently no position in the US Coast Guard that is not open to women, and that will soon be true for all branches of military service. The military is now in the process of opening itself up to equal opportunities for all members, regardless of sex or sexual preferences. The "Don't ask, don't tell" policy was appealed in 2011, which also allowed open gay marriages among military personnel.

As it currently stands, and it will probably not last long, as things are in a continuing state of change, almost day to day, same sex spouses receive the same benefits as traditional spouses, except for health benefits and housing. So, the military will truly be an equal opportunity employer. Time will tell how effective that will be. It makes absolutely no difference how any of us feel about the new policies; that is the way our world is today, and that is the way the military will go also.

Currently, and these figures change daily, women serve in about 91% of all Army occupations. Currently, 14% of the active Army is now composed of women and 23.2% of the Army Reserve is women. The figure for the Army National Guard is 13.3%. In all of the branches of service there are now 200,000 women, and the percentage of the overall structure is very similar to that of the Army. It is quite apparent that women play a significant role in the US military. They are very prominent in the Military Police, and have been for many years.

In Iraq and Afghanistan, as well as many other dangerous areas of the world, women have been in the forefront of hostile activities. They "man" Humvees, and fire machine guns right along with the men. They are on guard posts in hostile areas and provide convoy security. Although they have never before now been assigned to an infantry, armor or artillery line unit, they have still carried individual weapons and have been shot at just like their male counterparts. They have been wounded and killed, just like the men. Women are a large part of the Air Force fighter pilots running combat missions. Some have been shot down by enemy missiles. The press, however, frequently neglects to report all of those incidents, and the American public is sometimes not aware of many of those events. There have been many women who have received metals for valor, as high as the Silver Star, in combat areas. We do indeed have heroic women fighting in our ranks. Let us never lose sight of that fact.

New policies having been recently established, the controversy continues, just as it has for generations. Should men and women be in the same infantry roles, and in the same units to fight alongside one another? There are many arguments for and against the issue. One of the primary issues is the physical strength and endurance of females as compared with males. On average females, and these figures are not just for military women, are shorter and smaller than their male counterparts, with 40-50% less upper body strength and 25-30% less aerobic capacity, essential for endurance. There are times on the battlefield that we are called upon to hoist a wounded comrade on our shoulders and carry him to safety. What the average soldier must haul around with him every day while on an operation weighs in excess of eighty pounds. Are most women physically capable of those kinds of demands? At the same time, it is very evident that there are many women, despite the above figures and the required physical demands, who are more than capable of being effective soldiers. Physical capabilities are not the only determining factors, however.

The psychological differences between men and women could prove to cause some problems in the ranks. Many men feel that the traditional esprit de corps or camaraderie among the troops would be radically altered by adding women to the ranks. There is a bond that builds among men that might not be present with women in the same roles. They would have their own relationships among themselves, of course. The other problem that some see is the possibility of some bonding relationships going a different direction, toward the romantic side. That could definitely put a damper on the effectiveness of any military operation. There could never be room for romantic relationships in combat. It only works in the movies.

The effectiveness of a combat unit relies on the ability of each individual to be focused one hundred percent on the mission at hand. Romantic distractions could cause disasters and casualties. That could be a very real problem. The same, of course could be argued for accepting openly gay relationships in the military, and that, too, is a significant area of discussion. So, there it is. There is no way the military structure can control what goes on in the minds of its men and women, but it can control by means of regulations how we act toward one another. There are fewer sexual distinctions now than ever before, but whether or not sexual discrimination is still present remains to be seen. That is about as far as things have progressed at this point. We all stand in limbo, waiting for further developments, and we must continue to move right along.

Another psychological consideration is the psychology of the American people, who can only deal with so much of the reality of the atrocities that can happen in war. With women on the front lines of battle, there is always the possibility of their being captured and becoming prisoners of war, which has already happened at least once that has made news. It is bad enough when our men are captured and we at home have to deal with the abuses that we know they go through. There is a completely different psyche involved with the focus on women.

Even though there may or may not be sexual abuses to our men when in captivity, we generally do not give that possibility as much thought as we should. With women, there is a whole new set of criteria going on in our minds. Do we, as the supporters of our troops overseas in a combat environment, want to see our women subjected to that possibility? More than likely the answer will be an over whelming no. Most American have to face the fact that, generally speaking, we, as a people, see a difference between men and women, even though some female soldiers can be far superior to many male soldiers in every way, even in combat.

Several countries throughout the world have employed women in direct combat roles to include infantry. Israel is one country that has tried it. One of the things that they found was that when women were wounded or killed in action, it had a much more profound effect upon the male soldiers than when the same things happened to their male comrades. The trauma of witnessing the women suffering was more than many of them could handle, and therefore there was a tactical problem. The men, and therefore the unit, could not function effectively. They subsequently changed their policy back to not allowing women in direct combat roles. So, it was not the effectiveness of the women in combat, as that never really came into question. It was merely the fact that the men could not handle it well, but that is a reality that our combat forces must face now that we have adopted our current policy.

What the future will bring with the on-going dilemma over women in the military will without a doubt be extremely interesting and even exciting. Ladies, if you are up for becoming a part of some of the most controversial issues and some of the most significant changes ever in the military, now is a great time to get involved. Fantastic opportunities may be waiting for you to seize the moment. Change is in the air, and you can be a motivating part behind it. Are you up for it?

# Chapter 7 – Overseas Assignments

Although there are some close similarities between stateside assignments and overseas assignments, the contrasts are much more interesting and significant, and certainly worth discussion. These assignments also involve transitions, but the assignments themselves are important enough to discuss separately. Although our own country has a wide variety of cultural norms, America is still America, and wherever you may go, that fact will never change, nor would most of us ever want it to. When you travel the world, however, as all branches of the service require to some degree, you will experience cultures with norms that you have never imagined. If you have not already experienced such a thing, you are in for an education that you could never receive from any college or university alone. What you retain from books is extremely important, but it cannot measure up to what you experience first-hand in the real world.

I would never attempt to relate all the seemingly strange things that one can find in the vast array of cultures in the world, but one rather bizarre experience that comes to mind is right out of the Republic of South Vietnam. In the village of Lang Duk, previously mentioned, in which my company lived while in the Mekong Delta, I was acquainted with several of the locals. A relative of one of the people I knew died, and I was invited to the funeral. Not to offend the person, of course, I accepted the invitation. I had no idea what to expect, nor had I given it a great deal of thought beforehand. I merely arrived at the designated time and place. It was obvious to me right away that this was going to be like no funeral that I had ever seen before, and I had been to quite a number of them at home in the States, as young as I was at that time. I looked at it as another cultural experience.

The first thing I observed as I approached the funeral site was the fact that nearly everyone present was drunk or very close to it, and continuing to drink what appeared to be rice whiskey. I did not have to understand the language to understand what was going on. This must have been their way of easing the pain of a friend or relative who has just passed, and these people were certainly used to death, as it was continuously with them nearly every day of their lives in one form or another. Their country was in the middle of a war.

Now, we all understand the serious nature of a funeral. However, as badly as I might feel about it, the whole scenario was one of the funniest things I have ever experienced and through which I tried desperately to maintain my composure and keep a straight face. Someone had already dug the grave into which the casket would be lowered. I can only imagine how that must have gone, as I was not a witness to that phase of the operation. Shortly after I arrived, the pallbearers approached the casket to carry it over to the gravesite and lower it into the ground. Those "gentlemen" were so far gone with the effects of the rice whiskey that they could hardly find the handles on the casket, let alone lift it up all together and carry it in any semblance of order. You just have to try to visualize this calamity.

Try not to think in terms of a western funeral, where everyone is well dressed and in dark colors and looking very traditionally western. We're talking about the men in shorts, sandals with soles made of car tires, and "wife-beater" shirts. Most of the women wore either white shirts with black pants or muumuu type dresses and sandals. The pallbearers looked no different than the other men in attendance. Somehow, the six men managed to move the casket to the gravesite, not exactly at funeral cadence, nor in anything resembling order. As a matter of fact they were stumbling all over one another, now and then losing their footing, not quite dropping the casket, but not far from it.

There was some sort of funeral music playing, with drums and a type of wind instrument, but few participants or observers seemed to be paying much attention to it. As the pallbearers came within a few feet of the grave, they stopped, put the casket down and seemed to ponder the situation. I am quite sure that they were at least aware that they were in no condition to successfully lower that casket into the grave without losing it in their attempt. I could not help but wonder about that myself. "Are they really going to attempt this?" was my thought.

May wonders never cease! They finally made the decision to do just that. Two of the men jumped/slid/fell (whatever) into the grave in order to grab the casket, as the other four prepared to lower it into the ground. It looked very much like a suicide mission. My eyes widened as I watched in utter amazement at what was unfolding before me. The four men above, who were trying desperately to maneuver the casket into the ground, dropped it at least twice, retrieving it the best they could, thankful, I'm sure, that it did not break open spilling forth its contents.

The four gentlemen above the grave lowered the casket into a hole that was only big enough for the coffin itself, let alone the two very drunk men waiting patiently in the hole. The simplest of math can tell you that this just is not going to work. There is not space enough for one coffin and two men! However, do not ever think for a moment that these people did not have it all together. No, they did manage to accomplish the mission. I have no clue how they managed to lower that coffin onto those two men and get them out, and have them all survive. While watching with unbelieving eyes, I did not actually comprehend the magic unfolding there. My mind was obviously preoccupied with the utter hysteria of the moment. My insides were ready to split, repressing the laughter, but I too managed to survive and join in the "mourning." That was indeed the craziest funeral I have ever witnessed. It is fun, however, reminiscing about it.

Here in the US we are accustomed to being a country that has never been occupied or conquered by a foreign entity during our lifetime. We take for granted many things that people in other countries cannot. We can look back at some events that have involved death and destruction, such as Pearl harbor and most recently the 9-11 tragedy of 2001, but we have never had an occupying force within our country since the Revolutionary War; all right, maybe Mexico, if we really want to be technical. For freedoms from repression we can certainly be grateful, but, as a result of that, our attitudes are much different than those people who have witnessed, been a part of and remember such things.

One of my Army reserve tours took me to Germany for an annual training exercise called REFORGER (Redeployment of Forces to Germany) for about a month. I tried to convince the Army to save itself (as well as me) some money, and just leave me there after the exercise was over, because I was planning to spend some time there anyway. I was taking a year off work for that purpose. They would not hear of it. It would be against regulations to do it that way. So, a short time later I took my year off from teaching, and returned, that time at my own expense.

During my second visit, which was considerably longer, I was in the city of Kassel when a cathedral caught my eye. It was obvious to me that at one time in the past it had been a remarkable, beautiful structure, and had been badly damaged during World War II by American or British bombers. Rather than rebuilding the steeples, which had been damaged or destroyed, with an attempt at the original architectural style, the people of Kassel elected to refurbish it, not with that original style, but rather to rebuild it with what appeared to be a modern, aluminum-siding type of structure, which was, by far, the ugliest architectural structure that I had ever seen in my life, at least for an old cathedral. It was truly pitiful.

As I stood across the street from this rather obscene structure, just looking at it, there was an old, native German gentleman standing nearby. Having been a German teacher at the time, I chose to engage him in conversation, of course, in his own native language. I commented to him that I thought it was horrible the way they chose to reconstruct that church. I asked him why they did not choose to restore the original appearance.

His response surprised me. He told me that it was all very intentional. They made a statement by making it as ugly as it was, and he did not at all deny that fact, nor seem apologetic in any way. It was to be a memorial to the German people to remind themselves that they never again wanted to allow these kinds of atrocities to occur in their country. Judging from their politics since World War II, including removing the Berlin wall, and having never become involved in any world conflict since then, it would appear that they are indeed quite serious about avoiding war at any cost.

As Americans, we sometimes wonder why we seldom have the support from European countries that we feel we should have. It is not so much that what America does is so bad; it is just that the Europeans have been through so much, none of them desire to take those kinds of risks again. England, of course, remains the exception. They have continued their loyalty to the United States. Then again, they, just as America, have never been conquered and occupied, at least not in recent history. Thus, we see attitudes throughout the world that are much different from our own, and that is a very good thing, in that it enables Americans to have a more balanced perspective of the world.

There are also cultures throughout the world that are not all that different from our own, but that may or may not encourage us to spend a great deal of time there and away from our homeland. To avoid offending anyone, we will not mention any names, but, when they do come up, we know automatically which countries to avoid in our travels, if possible. Of course, today most want to avoid travel throughout many countries, due to so many terrorist activities, drug trafficking and anything else that may seem dangerous to the average traveler.

Beer drinking is an old American past time, but I would certainly hope that no one is naïve enough to think that we Americans invented either the beverage or the social event itself. On the contrary, the beverage had

its earliest origins in the Middle East, long before the
Middle Ages, and later, into the thirteenth century,
spread across Europe as mead and ale. All of this was
long before beer was even thought of in western
civilization. Again, we return to Germany where beer is
one of the cultural mainstays of the country. I am not
sure if any Americans or British ever thought of the idea
in World War I or World War II, but, if we creative
Americans or British had considered the idea of
bombing beer manufacturers in addition to military
targets, perhaps we could have ended the war much
sooner than we did. Kill the German beer, and you kill
the whole German culture! What were we thinking?

While in Germany, I spent a lot of time in Munich. I
love that city! It is one of the largest in Germany, but
one that conveys a small town environment and
atmosphere. There seem to be beer halls everywhere,
and, if I am not mistaken, it is the beer-drinking capital
of the world. I know that it is among the highest in the
number of alcoholics in the world, but that, of course, is
not what I like about it. What I observed in Munich was
beyond anything I have ever seen before anywhere in
the world. With absolutely gorgeous surroundings, being
in southern Bavaria, having the most beautiful examples
of antiquity and some of the true marvels of the modern
world, the people themselves were a sight to see, and it's
not like there was a stereotypical Bavarian in lederhosen
on every corner. On the contrary, it had one of the
widest varieties of people imaginable. What the people
were doing was much more important than how they

looked. Watching their habits was an education in itself. The variety of activities was part of the charm of the city.

There were indeed many Bavarians who looked like they could be from nowhere else but Bavaria, but most looked like anyone you would see in any major American city. Throughout the city there was a fabulous variety of cultural events going on all of the time. You could see science museums, art museums, concerts, opera, theater, and even movie theaters where you could see American movies dubbed in German or with German subtitles. Let us not neglect the cathedrals, the historical sights and the beautiful parks including the English Gardens, which was quite interesting, particularly in the summertime. At that time of the year dress was optional in the English Gardens and frequently constituted nothing at all. Sunbathing in the nude was quite acceptable, and it did catch me a bit off guard, as no one had previously warned me about what I might encounter. Possibly I missed something in the translation. Yes, I confess, that phenomenon did "catch my eye" also.

Returning to the subject of beer halls, however, I saw things in those establishments that were then and probably remain unprecedented. I have never seen such quantities of beer consumed by single individuals anywhere in my life. Some of those old Germans could put away ten or twelve liter-steins of beer in a single evening and walk away without even staggering. That would not be, however, without urinating all over the walls outside before departing the area. You can well imagine the smell outside the halls most of the time. The bar maids were also a sight to behold. Those ladies were usually rather robust, and some looked like they could have been football or rugby players for a local team. Many were quite small, and yet I would hate to challenge any one of them to an arm wrestling match. They would haul four or five liter-steins full of beer in each hand all the way across those huge beer halls, and they never looked like they were even a little bit tired. It was remarkable.

Another phenomenon I observed in many areas of the world is that of the use of bicycles, which would be a huge contrast to what one sees in the United States. At home in America we see children all over the country enjoying their little two-wheeled vehicles of recreation and sometimes transportation. Often we see adults using them for exercise, races, extreme sports, as well as recreation, and occasionally as a necessity. In other countries, particularly third-world countries, we see much more in the way of the bicycle being a normal mode of transportation. It is often the only means of transportation available to a family. In both Southeast Asia and Korea I have seen more bicycles than automobiles, more so in Southeast Asia, where the bicycle rickshaw is also still a major mode of transportation. The reasons should be pretty obvious if you think about the cost of operating a bicycle over operating a motor vehicle.

If you you've never witnessed it, you would not believe how high a person can pile or pack "crap" on top of a bicycle and still be able to control it. You may take that last statement either literally or figuratively, as the bicycle may well be stacked with bags of manure. The top of the "freight" could easily be twice the height of the person with the bike. If it were stacked that high, the person would probably not be trying to ride the bike, but rather just pushing it along the street. It was, nevertheless, something to remember for a very long time. Not only do you need to try to formulate that picture in your mind; try to add to it the same person with three or four cartons or baskets on top of his or her head. That would be two balancing acts at a time going on. For crying out loud, they could easily be in a circus, and be just as entertaining! But they are not doing it to entertain. That is the way they live every day of their lives. It is fascinating, however you look at it.

There are many people, admittedly or otherwise, who have within them prejudices that could very well affect the way they deal with unusual situations found in foreign countries. They need to be in touch with those feelings before going into an intolerable situation, one that would have significant effects on their ability to do their jobs, and represent the United States as ambassadors. For those who might have prejudices that are racial in nature, he or she might well have problems in their own neighborhoods, let alone in a foreign country. That person would have difficulty in South or Central America if they had problems with Hispanics.

They would have difficulty in Africa if they had problems with black people. Many today have problems with Muslims. They would find it very difficult in the Middle East. All such feelings must be dealt with before going into the military. There is no way that any of that can or will be tolerated. The military itself is multiracial, and, if a person has racial issues, then the military will not be able to use him or her in any way. Anyone with those kinds of feelings would be unsuitable for military life, and I would not recommend such an endeavor.

The vast array of world travel that the military offers is probably self-explanatory. It is an education all by itself. You see things during those travels that you would never be able to imagine. The world is so full of interesting cultures and ways of life that it opens up your mind to how the other parts of the world live. It broadens your horizons and gives whole new perspectives on how you view the world around you. After such exposure, you will have a much better understanding of how different peoples of the world think. Without those kinds of experiences, you are pretty much confined to an ethnocentric point of view, and your ability to think expansively is inherently limited. You cannot think beyond what the average American thinks, who has not been introduced to other cultures of the world. These are indeed growing experiences for all. A military life can provide that for you.

## CHAPTER 8 – CONFRONTING "OTHER" LIFE

I named this chapter as I did because of military people frequently going into areas of operation that few people in civilian life would ever venture. We run into wild life that would be an infrequent occurrence in most other walks of life. Those entering the military should be very much aware of many of the potential threats that are present throughout the world, many of which they might encounter. Thinking in terms of making the right decisions about the military as a choice of lifestyle, one must think beyond just the adventure, nuances, the quest for discovery and all the rest. What is it, if anything, that would render you incapable of functioning? Are you totally petrified by snakes, spiders or other creepy-crawly things, or large animals, like tigers, elephants, alligators, water buffalo or even camels?

If a person were to have serious problems with such things, then maybe reevaluating the whole idea of the military, or certain branches of it, might be in order. Would it bother a person terribly, to the point of being traumatized, to see a dog over an open-pit barbeque? In Southeast Asia dog is one of the main staples. There were very few dogs running around loose when I was there. The Viet Cong would snatch them up in a minute for a good meal. One must be prepared for all sorts of situations unheard of in the US.

As you have undoubtedly noticed, I tend to categorize many of my experiences in the military as the old "good, bad and ugly." I can't help it; I'm an old Eastwood fan. Many of the examples I use occur within training areas of US installations, but many go right into the field of operations, where you might well be working after all of your training is complete; out in the world, if you like. The next few incidents I categorize primarily as part of the bad and the ugly, and yet each of the bad experiences that most of us have contribute more than we can imagine to our overall character; hence, the good!

Throughout my military life I have had numerous encounters with life forms other than human. Why don't we just begin on the home front and then progress to international waters? Actually, to be quite honest, I only recall a couple of such incidents here in the United States, associated with the military, both of which involved our slithery, legless friends, the snakes. These two incidents were also at what I affectionately refer to as my home-away-from-home, Fort Benning, Georgia.

Snakes have really never been a major problem for me. I've never had any significant fear of them, and yet I do treat them with a healthy respect if I do not know who they are (venomous or non-venomous). I much prefer to deal with them on a one-on-one basis than one (me) against a large grouping of them, which brings up the first "close encounter." If I recall correctly, I was on a training patrol during my Infantry OCS, commonly referred to as "Benning's School for Boys." We were in a period of reduced visibility, as it was toward the end of the day. The area was heavy with thick brush and very rocky. As I climbed over a large rock outcropping, I suddenly froze in place!

Not more than five feet in front of me was the largest group or mass of snakes I've ever seen in my life (other than in some rather grotesque documentaries or Indiana Jones thrillers). There must have been thirty to fifty snakes (I didn't take the time to count them) all coiled around one another, slithering in one large mass of continuous movement. I had no idea at the time what type of snakes they were, but I was quite pleased that I had not taken one additional "(small step) for mankind." The result would not have been pleasant, even if those creatures had been totally harmless. I learned, however, that some of those situations that I had only seen on the screen actually can be observed in real life. That's a pretty creepy thought, right?

The second such incident was merely a one-on-one contact, and I knew my adversary quite well, which made it a bit simpler. The real problem was that he wanted to become even better acquainted with me than I with him; this time I was facing a water moccasin. I was nearly waist-deep in water at the time, which was not a plus for me, and it was also my "friend's" domain, and he was right at home on his own "turf." I was the intruder. That reptilian "creature from the Black Lagoon" was, reality told me, and my imagination exaggerated for me, headed directly toward my crotch, mouth wide open, as he progressed toward me.

Each moment that elapsed showed another segment of my life passing before my eyes. What a way to go! I had an M-16 rifle with me, but this was a training situation, and blank ammunition is not terribly effective against live enemy targets, and that cottonmouth was a well-defined enemy, even though I affectionately referred to him as "friend." The most reasonable thing I could think of to do was make an honorable, retrograde movement (i.e., retreat), swinging my rifle butt and attempting a good vertical butt stroke. I'm happy to report that I broke contact with my would-be attacker, but not before he tightened the old "pucker factor" on me just a bit. I can hardly imagine how I would have reacted if I had had a fear of snakes. I had a significant respect for them however, which was growing at that particular moment.

Leaving the comforts of home in the US, I went on a short "vacation" to the Isthmus of Panama for a two-week course called J.O.C. (Jungle Operations Course). The Army, in all its wisdom, decided that this course would prepare me for the jungles of Vietnam and make me a true jungle fighter, or "Jungle Expert," as the patch reads. There was nothing further from the truth, but, hey, it was fun and it gave me a break from what I was doing, which was not all that enjoyable. I have always called it the Army's gentleman's course, particularly when compared to Ranger School. In truth, I encountered very little in the way of wild life there, interesting as the area was. Indeed, the plant life was more interesting than the animal life. I recall very clearly a nice little plant called black palm. Each plant looked like a sea urchin with poisonous spines about six inches long sticking out from the main trunk of the tree. I managed to avoid a direct encounter with them fortunately, but many of my fellow students were not so lucky, and, I was told that direct contact results in some of the most excruciating pain one could ever imagine.

There was one particular situation with which I was confronted that would probably be of more interest to the city slicker, rather than the country person. At that early stage in my life, I was much more the former than the latter. One part of J.O.C. (and, I might add, the best part) was the E and E (escape and evasion) course. It was a three-day event, and the object was to escape from and evade the aggressor or opposition forces, and survive on whatever you could. We were given very little in the way of food or drink, but one of the items we were given was a live chicken! As I recall, we did not keep the chicken all that long before deciding to kill and eat it. Let's face it, trying to be as quiet as possible in order to evade enemy captors is tough enough. Try adding a live chicken and keeping it quiet as you move with stealth through the darkness and quiet of the jungle. So, we had at least one good meal fairly early through the E&E course.

I had the honor of "preparing" the chicken for dinner. The first question I had to ask myself was, of course, "How is an old city-slicker like me supposed to kill this rather harmless chicken?" The most logical thing to do, it seemed to me, was to grab it by the head and start swinging it in jerky circles in order to break its neck. It seemed the least inhumane method at any rate, and it worked, gruesome as it was. That wasn't quite gruesome enough, however, as we then had to skin it. That worked pretty well also, although I doubted I would ever have an occupation in a slaughterhouse, and I never did.

Another animal incident occurred in the Republic of Vietnam sometime in late 1967 or early 1968. I was an infantry platoon leader, and my platoon was on a very routine "search and clear" operation. In route to our objective, we ran across a small herd of water buffalo. As we approached the animals, they seemed to have no inclinations to allow us to pass. American troops know that killing domestic animals is not in the picture at all. However, one of my over-zealous young troops decided to display his apparent "great white hunter" image and unload a twenty-round magazine from his M-16 rifle into one of the buffalo.

What a sight! The water buffalo with twenty rounds of ammunition in his body just stood there, stared at the man, and did not move a muscle! The animal may well have dropped dead later in the day, but not at that moment. I have always felt for that poor, dumb animal, and I genuinely hope that he did not die, but we had no recourse but to leave the animal where he was and continue on with the mission. This certainly could well be interpreted as a total lack of self-discipline on the part of my young trooper! It certainly could have gone much worse for him as well as the rest of us. These are domestic animals, belonging to local farmers. That would have been a significant loss for a farmer, and that was also a good reason for my being so angry with that soldier of mine. We never heard any more about the incident.

The insect world is also part of the animal kingdom. I have some memorable experiences in that area, but for now, let's just deal with the Republic of Vietnam. Only in the old classical cartoons with Donald Duck, among others, have I ever seen mosquitoes as large and vicious as those I encountered in that part of the world. It was bad enough having to worry about all the two-legged adversaries out there trying to kill us every day. To make it worse, the mosquitoes were constantly trying to drink themselves into oblivion on human blood, primarily mine, or so it seemed.

Most of us have seen the cartoons where the mosquitoes, as big as dragonflies, zero in on their victim from ten feet up and dive-bomb them until they strike and penetrate deeply into the flesh. It all seems pretty funny in the cartoons, but there is actually a great deal of realism in that little scenario, considering that those little varmints really are out there doing exactly that, and they did it hundreds of times to nearly every soldier in the field. They were absolutely huge and you could actually hear them zeroing in on you, and "zap" they would get you! Mosquito repellant was an absolute must at all times, and I practically took a bath in the stuff several times each day, and even more at night. Whenever possible at night, I slept with a mosquito net covering me. That is just a part of life in the tropics.

Another really vicious, little creature that I encountered in Southeast Asia was the red, fire ant, not that I should be using that name in the singular, because there really were "tons" of them or billions, maybe literally. I remember one operation in particular, where we had a very long way to travel, too far even for us "hard-as-nails" infantrymen to walk. One leg of our mission was to travel by river on a Navy LCM (landing craft medium), operated by South Vietnamese Navy personnel. Those are the big, rectangular, flat boats with a big ramp in front from which to unload the troops onto a beach, or embankment, as was the case with us. The Marines used them in World War II. That's how old much of the equipment was that we used.

Anyway, at the end of that segment of the operation, we landed on a bank of the river where we were to continue on foot. As soon as we hit the embankment, we dropped the ramp and moved out onto the land, which was covered with palm growth. We had not moved more than a few feet before realizing that we were right in the middle of a fire ant colony! Wow! It's a very good thing that we did not come into immediate contact with Charlie, because we had a very formidable enemy already confronting us at the moment. I think every man in my platoon, myself included, was covered with biting red ants, and we had to literally strip down and pick those nasty-attitude critters off individually, but only after having to take the time to move out of that ant-infested area, thus allowing even more of the ants to crawl up onto our bodies. That was tough, painful and time-consuming, adding to our difficulties, as we had a mission to accomplish within a designated time.

There was a second incident also involving fire ants, which was again on an operation, the details of which are very foggy and not of any great significance. We were in view of the only mountain that could be seen for miles. To my best recollection, it was northwest of Saigon, in Tay Nin Province and the mountain was called Nui Ba Den or the Black Virgin Mountain. My company commander (it may have been the battalion commander) decided to go up onto that mountain to spend the night. It seemed like a fairly secure place. We arrived at our nighttime position, and set up a defensive position for the night. It was pitch black; so dark that we could not see our hands in front of our faces. I found a place to establish my platoon headquarters and within that area I discovered that I had placed myself in the vicinity of a couple of trees that were very close to one another.

Those two trees reminded me that several weeks before, someone had given me a hammock which rolled up to about the size of a baseball and fit neatly into my rucksack. I had never before used it and it seemed like a good opportunity on this particular night. I just happened to have a couple of trees at hand to which I could secure that hammock. Well, when it was time to sack out, I brought out the hammock, fumbling around blindly tying it to both trees, and climbed in. It felt great! It was much better than sleeping on the ground, to which I was certainly accustomed. A couple of hours later I awoke feeling like my entire body was on fire. Fire ants had approached (attacked) from both of the trees to which I had tied my hammock, and they were literally all over me. Again, I had to strip naked, pulling each of those horrible little critters off my body, one by one. Wow, those guys sure left marks! That's another memory I'll take to the grave.

I certainly would be remiss if I were to neglect my other old friends from the jungles of Southeast Asia, the leeches. You very frequently hear about leeches in swamplands and marshes, but that is not where I, with many others, encountered them. As many times as I, with my platoon, found myself in water from ankle-deep to neck-deep and beyond, I do not recall frequently finding leeches from those areas, although it did happen to others on many occasions. The infrequency was probably because most of the watery areas we were in had a salt content, and I don't think leeches do well in salty water. My own encounters were mostly from walking through the jungles. These were the type of leeches that maneuver along the ground like an inchworm, as they only have feet in the front and rear of their bodies. They can move very rapidly, however, particularly when they are hungry for that good rich blood, and that seemed to be most of the time.

The most memorable encounter with the leeches was the first time I had ever even seen one, let alone having a whole family or social group attached to my body. I had no warning about the possibility of running across any of these little gems. I had my fatigue trouser legs secured to my legs by blousing rubbers, just above the top of my boots, and I soon learned that that was not at all a good idea; certainly not for jungle terrain. See? JOC had not quite turned me into a jungle expert. We stopped our forward movement for a short break, and I felt a little itching sensation on one of my legs. Upon inspection, I found about a half dozen leeches attached to that leg, just above the top of my boot, and they were having a great lunch. Looking at the other one, I found nearly the same situation. It had turned into a banquet. That was not a pretty picture.

I immediately had my entire platoon check their own legs, and, as I anticipated, many of them found themselves in the same situation. We immediately stripped our boots and socks off, and began removing the leeches. There were two ways to do it; by burning them off with lit cigarettes, or, for non-smokers, like me, with insect repellent. Both methods worked well, but we still had nice little holes where each had attached itself. Each of those holes, for all of us, became infected, and, even though they continued to heal, they itched terribly for a couple of months thereafter. As each bite became infected, it had to be treated. For a long time, it seemed like it would never stop. Oh, our fun just never ceased!

There is one additional sweet little creature that I have yet to mention, and yet some people would think that I am crazy to have negative feelings about them. Children even have them as pets, as did my own sons. Those would be the rats. I hate rats! Vietnam had its fair share of them. That was not such a big deal to me until one night in the village when "Mother Nature" called, and I really had to go. The facility for such an occasion was an out-house type of structure at the end of a dock overhanging a major canal. It was a fair walk from where I lived, and it was dark. I hardly went anywhere without my personal weapon, this being no exception; being dark, I also had a flashlight. I began doing what I went there for, and in just a few minutes I heard a very strange little tapping sound, like the "pitter patter" of very little feet. Considering the purpose for which I was at the end of the dock, I began to become a little jittery. I was enshrouded by darkness, and completely alone, or so I thought.

Something else seemed to be on its way out to greet me. I grabbed my flashlight and turned it on. Twenty to thirty feet from me there were beady little eyes coming toward me; more than just a couple. I'm guessing that there were five or six rats coming out to make my acquaintance for whatever reason! I certainly could not start shooting them. I was right in the village, and I could have killed someone. All I could do is bang my flashlight on the wood planks in hopes of scaring them off. It worked, but not without scaring the crap out of me, if you'll pardon the expression. I had been in a very vulnerable position to be attacked by rats! Many years later my sons could not understand why I had no use for their pet rats. Hey, what could I tell them? These rats were wild in more ways than one, and the situation was pretty crazy.

## Chapter 9 – Wild And Crazy Things

Although the extremely serious nature of the military as a career or lifestyle choice should never be diminished or ignored, leaving it at that does not give anything close the complete picture of that lifestyle. There is a lighter side that goes along with the profession. There is a very old saying by which I try to live my life, and that is, "All work and no play make Jack a dull boy." There is a significant philosophy behind that saying. Particularly for a job that causes as much stress at times as the military can, there needs to be an outlet where one can relax for a while and forget about all of the stresses that go along with the job. The military provides an ample amount of that. Most people who have been in the military for any length of time can attest to the fact that there are some "wild and crazy" things (to quote Steve Martin) that happen throughout that life. It is one of the elements that would probably be responsible for many of us in the military to maintain our sanity and composure. That is why this subject is so terribly important to convey. It is part of the balance of such a life. We should also understand that many of those wild and crazy events are not necessarily entertaining, but nevertheless do break up any possible monotony that may on occasion go with the territory.

To begin the subject with a pretty wild adventure, and with no regard to chronological order, let's start with my flight to the Republic of (south) Vietnam. I was just coming off a brief leave from a short assignment at Fort Polk, Louisiana, and a quick visit home in San Diego. I had to go to Travis Air Force Base north of San Francisco for my departure. It was an early morning departure and the whole flight time, including a stop at Wake Island, an airstrip out in the middle of the Pacific somewhere east of the Philippines, was about nineteen hours. After a quick refueling, we were off again, directly to Vietnam. The pilot had informed us shortly after leaving Travis Air Force Base that our initial destination in South Vietnam was an airfield at Bien Hoa, arriving about 3:30 in the morning. Even before we landed at Wake Island, he had come back over the loudspeaker to inform us that Tan Son Nhut, the final destination, had been changed to Pleiku, about 200 miles north of Saigon. It's not like we knew where we were going or what to expect anyway; so, who really cared, right?

A few hours after leaving Wake Island, we had another announcement from the cockpit that there was another change of plans; we were now heading once again for Bien Hoa! As we continued our flight, as though we did not already have enough on our minds about what our immediate future had to offer, the flight crew kept us informed, step by step, as to the developments on the ground where we intended to land. That became increasingly uncertain as time went on.

We progressed toward Bien Hoa, and, as time passed, it seemed that there was intensifying enemy activity in progress right about where we had intended to set down. The crew was quite good at keeping our "pucker factors" right where they needed to be. At Tan Son Nhut, near Saigon, our newly designated landing site, there seemed to be a rocket or mortar attack in progress, and it was decided that it would not be in any of our best interests to land at that particular time and place. That too let up and we actually did land there. Well, we were not entirely sure we even wanted to exit the aircraft, but everything turned out fine. I am still not convinced that they don't put the "green" troops through all that nonsense just for effect, or even for their own entertainment. I've heard other very similar stories from other people; nearly identical stories!

I sometimes think that landing us right in the thick of things might have been the very best indoctrination possible for all newly arriving soldiers. However, I don't think the Air Force guys would be entirely sold on that concept. Was the entire scenario a staged deal for us? Who knows? I have some suspicions however. Possibly it was a way to show us that the training was over; it was now time for the real thing. If that were the case, it worked quite well. I think I was prepared for just about anything after that flight.

I'm not sure whether I would have preferred a daytime arrival into the country or a nighttime arrival. I arrived at night. Some came in during the daylight hours. To see or not to see; that is the question. Do you really want to see what's coming up, or do you want it to be a big surprise? Either way the imagination can go wild. From several thousand feet up some might have seen nothing at all unusual in their approach. Those would either have to presume that all this war "stuff" was a bunch of hype, or, of course, they could imagine the very worst happening. In any case, reality had not quite presented iteself.

Adding to the stress level just described, the normal flight procedures for aircraft landing at airstrips in Vietnam were not what most of us expected. Just before landing, and from an elevation of several thousand feet, the plane would take an extremely steep dive to the runway, which actually seemed like the aircraft had lost power and was just dropping to its final doom! Hey, upon arrival, we were all going to die!

Why would anyone have wanted to warn us about that part of the flight anyway? That was part of the excitement of the arrival. I am also sure the flight crew absolutely loved the reactions of all of the unsuspecting troops. How else were they supposed to entertain themselves with all of these back-to-back trips? If they hadn't been able to add some humor to it all, it could have been very depressing. After all, everyone was quite aware that many of these people were never coming back, except in a body bag.

Hostile fire areas are not the only places that these wild and crazy things occur. Try going through airborne training. Some extremely wild things can happen there.

The first week is rather boring compared to what comes the next two weeks. The first week is all about physical training; a good deal of running, push-ups, the daily dozen and the like. The next week is jump-tower week, which can be pretty exciting, but then comes the real excitement; the week for jumping from aircraft! That is what everyone has been waiting for, of course. You are more than ready to stand in the door, or at the rear ramp, with the world twelve hundred feet or more beneath you and the wind blowing wildly in your face, and the jump master ready to tap you on the shoulder. I speak for myself, because I was usually the guy standing in the door, the first to jump. I was a captain at the time, and it was generally the ranking individual who was first to go. But all of us are pumped!

Wait a minute. Don't jump the gun here. Obviously, the flight crew is not quite ready; the red light is still on, and nobody is going anywhere until it turns green. You wait and wait, wondering what's going on. The jumpmaster is in touch with the pilot and he tells us that there is too much wind on the ground and he is not satisfied that it would be safe to drop us. Time goes on and it is getting pretty late; almost time for dinner. The aircraft crewmembers are getting hungry and their families are expecting them home soon. I am sure what's going through the pilot's mind is, "Oh, to hell with them! Drop these sorry bastards, and let's get out of here." The green light comes on. You remember the cadence you have been singing on most of your runs: "Stand up, hook up, shuffle to the door; jump right out and count to four." Your stomach muscles tighten, the hair on the back of your neck stands up like a wire brush, you move awkwardly toward the door, your body shaking all over, and the jump master slaps your shoulder; out you go! "One thousand, two thousand, three thousand, four thousand…" (normally the count that it takes for a parachute to fully deploy). You feel a nice strong tug, look up and see a wonderful sight: a full canopy; a truly heart-warming sight.

There is nothing now but the dead silence of the open space, except for that wonderful soft breeze whispering by your ears. Your descent feels so slow and relaxing. This is the most relaxed that you have ever felt in your life. You feel like you could remain up here for eternity, but that is highly unlikely. Your descent continues, and you notice that the ground seems to be coming up to meet you a little faster by the second. Also of interest is the fact that, as well as the ground coming up a little faster, the ground seems to be moving a great deal faster horizontally than you might have expected. This may not be a good thing. Actually, it is getting a little scary. It is not at all just your imagination. It's for real. Your chute is beginning to oscillate with the wind, and the ground is coming to meet you even more quickly than before and there is no way you are going to slow it down. Your chute oscillates right with the wind as you come closer to hitting the ground at probably thirty-five to forty miles per hour.

You try desperately to remember the five points for a good PLF (parachute landing fall); balls of feet, calf, thigh, buttocks, push-up muscles, and "crash!" So much for that idea. Try feet, butt, head, and you keep right on going with the wind. You feel like you are out on the water behind a ski boat, skimming along on your chest, but it hurts a great deal more. As the thirty-five mile-per hour wind carries you along the uneven ground, all you can think about, as you try desperately to find that quick-release strap you learned about in the first or second week of training, is that tree stump that is about to slam into your chest! The imagination once again can be a killer here. Finally, you find the quick-release and the chute collapses, and again you are safe and very relieved, though quite bruised just about everywhere. So, get up, you freakin' idiot, gather your chute and double-time off the drop zone to turn in your chute! Now, wasn't that first jump all that you expected and more? Hey, fear not; it's great fun!

Don't be discouraged yet; I'm on a roll. I have at least a couple more for you. There's nothing like the night jump, especially when it is an equipment jump, as most are. Now and then they might give us a "Hollywood jump," which is just the jumper and his parachute, but those are rare. In addition to our parachutes (both the regular chute and our reserve), we have the rest of our equipment, all of which is attached to our bodies, and off we go to our aircraft. Our equipment weighs about an additional fifty or sixty pounds, and we look a little silly, hauling all this stuff around like third-world country peddlers carrying their goods off to market. Anyway, our aircraft leaves the ground, and off we go again into the blackness of the night sky. This time it's much cooler, and I'm not referring to the weather. In a sense I am, as thunder and lightning accompany us, just to make it less quiet, dark and lonely up there.

I have to admit that we are not right in the middle of the thunderstorm. It is far off in the distance, but how good is one's sense of distance at night at twelve hundred feet up? Anything is worth a chance when it is this fun, right? Of course, right. Again, stand up, hook up, shuffle to the door, but this time we are about to jump blindly into the darkness of the night with no clue as to where we will be "landing," if that will be the most appropriate term. It could be on nice, level, dry terra firma, or it again could be something that we don't even want to think about, but, of course, we do. Could it be a water landing, one of those infamous tree landings that you have heard about so often, or might you just land in a deep hole in the ground, or on a "BFR" (that would be a big rock)? You are out of the plane, having counted to four, and for a split second you wonder about that full canopy which has not quite opened. It took just a tad longer to open with fifty or so extra pounds. Whew! There's that reassuring tug, and, yes, there is the canopy.

So far, so good. Again, you are having a nice, slow, relaxing descent to the ground. By the way, where is the ground? You know that it has to be down there somewhere, but damned if you can see it! Thank goodness for that lightning, because now and then it flashes just enough to allow you a brief glimpse of the ground just to reassure you that it really is there. On the other hand, it is not all that cool to think about being barbequed by that lightning that keeps you aware of its presence. There is actually a third "hand" here; there are not quite as many lightning flashes as you would like to have, as you are still not sure just when you will be meeting up with the ground. By the way, you may well be thinking entirely too much here. Have you lost track of the fact that the ground should be coming up any – "Ahh, shit!" Well, there it was, just a bit earlier than you thought it would be! If it were not for all of that equipment that you forgot to release before you hit, you might just have killed yourself! It broke your fall.

I am sure you have surmised that these examples that I am giving you are true-life events of the author. Then again, some of my readers, who have gone through the Army's Airborne School, have gone through some very similar events. I have to end this section of airborne training on the previously mentioned, infamous tree landing, because, yes, I was one of those lucky fellows who happened to have had that experience.

Long after those Army airborne experiences, as an assistant store opener with store development in a discount store chain, I frequently gave our opening crews their safety briefings. I would tell them, "If there is any accident that can possibly happen to you while you are working for us, I want you to know that I have been there and done it. I am the company expert on accidents and being in the wrong places at the wrong times." They could always come to me for any consultation on the subject. Don't get the wrong impression. I was not accident prone. Perish the thought. I was merely the victim of circumstances beyond my control. Gee, I'm glad I cleared that up for you.

All right, here we go again with another jump! That is always so exciting that I can hardly express myself. The same routine; up we go with all the confidence in the world that the US Air Force will once again deliver us on time and on target at the drop zone. Don't ever let them fool you. They are not that good! Sorry about anything offensive I might say or imply. I can only relate the facts of my own experiences. The jumpmaster is getting us prepared for the jump. We see our green light, stand up, hook up and out we go: "Geronimo!" I have that comforting tug, a beautifully deployed canopy, gorgeous blue sky, and a nice gentle breeze. What could be better? It has to be the perfect jump.

I begin looking around to see where I am headed and where I want to end up. I detect a little trouble on the horizon. "Houston, we have a problem." There does not seem to be a drop zone – anywhere. I mean, I look to the front; I look to the rear; I look to both sides; nothing but trees as far as the eye can see. Yes, indeed, we have a problem. Let's try to analyze this situation just a bit. I'm sorry. What is it we're analyzing here? There is only one reason that we cannot see a drop zone. There is no drop zone! These Air Force aeronautical geniuses, and I would have to include our Army jumpmaster, would have to take the rap on this one.

I also want to point out that not all Air Force pilots and Army jump masters fit into this category of inept people in the military, but these guys actually missed the drop zone! For crying out loud, the drop zone is two miles wide and three miles long! How in the world can you miss a target that big? Who knows and who really cares at this point? All we have to do now is find a piece of dirt with which to make contact. Nice plan, but all I see is trees, trees and more trees. There does not seem to be even a small clearing anywhere toward which to maneuver with the limited steering capabilities of this chute.

Well, after such an extensive analysis, it would seem that there is but one solution. Go with the flow (literally), close your eyes and pray. That was about it, and I remember that short prayer; it went very much like, "Ready or not, Lord, here I come!" I saw the trees (no ground, mind you) coming up to greet me (and, yes I was quite aware that I was actually going down to meet them) and there was little I could do but brace for impact. I counted down, as I recall: three, two, one, "crash, crunch, snap," and I blacked out for a few moments. I opened my eyes and was looking straight up into the sky through numerous branches and leaves. I also noticed that I could not seem to move at all. My entire body was immobile for some reason. I then noticed that both arms and both legs were bound to tree limbs by my parachute suspension lines.

This could have been the closest I have ever felt physically to Jesus Christ, bound to the cross. By no means would I ever want to sound sacrilegious, as I really am a true believer, but honestly, as I was sprawled out in that tree, I was extremely vulnerable to just about anything, and I was not at all sure whether or not death was hovering close by.

I tried to figure out how to extract myself from this ridiculous mess, and after ten or fifteen minutes I managed to loosen the lines wrapped about my body, but not without having to cut many of them. It would have made it a great deal easier to slide down out of that tree by means of partially repelling, had all of my lines still been intact and uncut. It's true that I did very little correctly on that jump.

After having freed myself from my bindings, and being more than ready to descend from the tree, I noticed a big CH-47 Chinook helicopter flying over-head, the crew trying to spot jumpers in the trees. One of the spotters, hanging out of the back window of the chopper, noticed me, and that huge helicopter began to drop down toward my tree and me. This young buck, enthusiastic as can be and obviously pleased that he had spotted me, directed the pilot a little closer for a good look at my rather precarious situation. That was not at all a good idea. My tree caught the prop-wash from the two giant blades of the helicopter, and my tree began to sway, as though in hurricane force winds. After having survived that tree fall, I knew it was all over for me now. The helicopter that was sent to rescue me was going to kill me, right there in front of God and everyone! I knew that for sure. I just said once again, "All right, Lord, we have been through this more than once; if this is it, get ready for me; here I come!"

I was trying desperately to wave off the helicopter, while that young man inside was waving to me. Finally, the pilot got the message and apparently decided that it would not be a great idea to let me die in front of them. Now this guy was an Army pilot, not Air Force (just wanted to clarify). He abruptly veered off and I was safe for the moment.

My next step was to try to remove myself from the tree. It was probably close to a hundred feet to the ground from where I was. I would have to descend branch by branch to reach the ground. It went quite well actually until I reached about thirty feet from the bottom. I then noticed that there was a conspicuous lack of branches. From that point, it was more like a telephone pole than a tree. I did not have my pole-climbing boots on; so, I pretty much had to do it the hard way. I began my slow slide down the branchless tree. It did not remain slow, however. From that point, for all practical purposes, I lost it. Down I went, full speed. I hit very hard, and noticed that my hands looked and felt pretty much like raw hamburger. I won't go into detail about any other body parts. I was, nevertheless, quite happy that I had made it, all in one piece, and I was ready to go again! Airborne!

I am sure that every branch of the service has its wild and crazy things happen, many of which probably make my examples look pretty minor. I had a lot of fun with most of mine, as long as there was no one trying to kill me. There was one that probably could have gone either way, I suppose, but several of us really enjoyed taking full advantage of an opportunity. Again allow me to take you back to the Mekong Delta, where, for the most part, it was not always a great deal of fun, but now and then things happen.

One day, with little or no warning, we received a neat little package (not that little actually), which was apparently to be used as an experimental combat model, for lack of another term, to see if it would be effective as a weapons system in our area of operations. It was a swamp boat with a huge fan on the back, the type you would see in the bayous of Louisiana. We could not believe our eyes! Was this some kind of elaborate Army joke, or was the Army really trying to break up the pressures of combat by giving us some recreational activity? One interesting addition to this recreational "toy" was a 50-caliber machine gun to be mounted on the front, which seemed to decrease the recreational properties.

Sometimes you just have to bite the bullet (yes, .50 cal. bullets are tough on the teeth) and do what you have to do. We were required to train with this new "weapon" and see how effective against our delta adversaries it could be. Wow, did we train! We would cruise through those rice paddies at forty-five or fifty miles per hour, flying over the dykes, having more fun than you could possibly imagine for being in a hostile fire area. We were without a doubt not as cautious as we should have been in our training, but we sure had fun. That is probably why we had to give it up after a very short time. We never made enemy contact while using that boat; so, although it is only my opinion, I do not think we were given a fair chance to really evaluate the weapon. What a pity. We gave it our best shot (a well thought out pun, of course). It was great while it lasted. After we gave it up, we never saw that "weapons system" again.

Speaking of weapons systems, and considering my comments concerning unit readiness on the first page of this book, I really did have some "close encounters of the first kind" with tanks, and I also mentioned that I was a tank company commander for a short time with the California Army National Guard. Most of our weekend drills were out in the desert east of San Diego at Fort Irwin, which later became the Army's national desert training center. It used to be strictly for reserve component units. We had all of our permanent equipment stored out there and we would travel by bus to the desert every month, leaving Friday evening and returning on Sunday.

Granted, being an old grunt (infantry) officer, I was not well trained on tanks, but for a period of time I received some significant hands-on training with the M-48A1 tank, all fifty-two tons of it. I had the opportunity to fire the main gun, as well as the .50 caliber machine gun, and had ample opportunity to drive the vehicle at break-neck speeds across the California deserts. It was awesome! Converting a massive weapons system like that into what I could not help but consider a recreational vehicle was fantastic! That was an ORV without comparison. I had the chance to drive it at over fifty miles per hour down a dirt road and across the open desert, maybe a little slower now and then, yet astonishingly fast.

No amusement park could ever come close to matching the excitement of that experience. On the other hand, again being very accustomed to the infantry, I personally would never have wanted to take one of those babies into combat; I considered them to be coffins on tracks, with missiles controlling today's battle field. A hit is a kill on the modern battlefield, and I for one would rather take my chances hiding behind a rock. All right, I can't brag all that much about my heroic qualities, not that I ever claimed to be a hero.

One of the wildest activities while in Vietnam, and I am sure the situations in Iraq, Afghanistan, Africa, South America or anywhere else in the world we might end up would be no different, was flying around in helicopters. All of the helicopter pilots I ran across in Vietnam were Army, and most were a real trip. I often thought that there must have been a prerequisite for the Army's flight school; you had to be little nuts prior to acceptance. Most of those folks were well trained and great at what they did, but they could also curl your hair at times.

Generally the chopper pilots flew the way they did for good reason. It was a matter of survival for themselves and their crews, as well as protecting whoever their passengers were, usually US Army personnel. More often than not, their routine flights from point A to point B were more fun than the greatest of amusement park rides in America, presuming that no one was shooting at you. Helicopters are prime targets for the bad guys; that is as true today as it was in the Vietnam War. We have been losing our people left and right in Iraq and Afghanistan, not only on the ground, but also from terrorists and other combatants shooting our aircraft out of the air. Things very frequently do not change much over long periods of time. It is more lethal now, as ground-to-air missiles are more dangerous than RPG rockets, which were primarily what we had to deal with forty or fifty years ago, and, yes, we still contend with them today.

Getting back to "Mr. Toad's Wild Ride," however, the pilots would fly fast and low most of the time, and, when they did fly high, much like our fixed-wing aircraft, they would go nearly vertical until they reached their required altitude in order to minimize their vulnerability and exposure time to enemy fire. The same would apply to dropping from a high elevation to low-level flying; the chopper would drop like a rock! Your stomach would seem like it went all the way up into your throat. At low-level flight they would cruise at just above treetop level, seemingly brushing those treetops, and, when they made a turn, it would be at nearly a right angle. The chopper would be with its right or left side nearly straight down. We were usually sitting in bench seats or sitting on the floor with our legs dangling out the side of the aircraft; forget about seat belts or closed doors. If it were not for centrifugal force, we would have been falling out of the helicopters to certain death. But then, that's what real fun is all about, right?

Hey, I loved that, honestly. I almost feel like I have to apologize for making a combat zone seem like Disneyland, but really there was much more to combat tours than killing, with all of the blood and gore, and other horrible things that do happen in combat. You look for the brighter sides, and, whenever you can find them, you cherish them, and remember them forever. Some may call that denial, but honestly it is much more pleasant to highlight the lighter side than the darker, more dismal side. And, of course, I enjoy telling about that part.

I already covered the incident in Vietnam with the hand grenade popping out of the hole. Yes, that was pretty crazy, but way back, long before the "real stuff," in advanced infantry training, right after basic, there was that ever-so-thrilling hand grenade training. That was always pretty scary for people who hardly knew a hand grenade from a pineapple. On the practice ranges, however, there was probably very little difference. The practice grenades were inert (no explosive material inside) and did not taste anything like pineapples. We actually did become reasonably proficient at throwing them.

After a few hours on the practice range it was time to go to the live hand grenade range. Even though we had had a few classes on throwing the practice grenade, it did not mean we were experts at throwing a live hand grenade. Without trying to justify our rather low level of training, I am not sure how much more effective that training could have been. We knew the killing radius of the exploding grenade and about how far we could probably throw it under ideal conditions, which would include not being nervous. We had thrown several dummy grenades, which, of course, were empty of all the explosive material, therefore making them lighter, and we were able to throw them farther than the real ones. We also knew that they could not explode; so, why would we even be nervous or concerned in any way? However, when you stand on a range with a real one in your hand, your mind can go crazy thinking about all the things that can go wrong, which your drill instructor has explained extensively for you in rather gruesome detail.

That little laundry list could go on forever. You could stumble on your attempted throw; the thing could slip out of your hand at any point; you could catch part of it on your shirt; there could be an obstacle in front of you that you hit, and the grenade bounces back at you. I could go on, but you get the point. Far too many people have been accidentally killed on the hand grenade range. Not only does the thrower of the grenade have to be continuously aware of everything going on, but the lane grader (individual supervisor out there with the thrower) has to be even more aware of what's going on. One minor slip-up and several people could be killed or seriously injured.

All of those horrible possibilities are raging in the soldier's head, and that is exactly why those accidents happen. Is there any way of avoiding that sort of scenario? Not really; the soldier must function in a real life situation under the same pressures. I gave the real life example of the grenade incident earlier in the book. Again, that is just part of that wild and crazy, yet very serious game, of learning the best ways to kill. What can I say? That may sound a bit gruesome, but that really is what the combat arms are all about. That's our job; that's what we do.

Besides all those "in the line of duty" wild things, there are also things that are available to military people in their off-duty hours. While I was stationed at the Presidio in sunny California, we had a nice four-day weekend coming up. I was talking to a couple of friends about what we might do for that long weekend. The subject of Hawaii came up and we began to think about the possibilities. Being active military, we had a few opportunities unavailable to most people, and being somewhat cocky young officers, we probably had a bit more initiative than other "normal" people might have had, and thought we might very creatively pull something off. We made arrangements through our travel section to fly out of Travis Air Force Base on board an Air Force cargo plane carrying a water purification unit to Vietnam. It was to stop off at Honolulu on the way. We were ready for it! At that point we had no idea what type of aircraft on which we would be flying, but why would we care? It was all free.

When we left San Francisco, heading north to Travis Air Force Base, we were dressed in our class A greens, the dress uniform, not having thought about what sort of flight accommodations we might find. Boarding the aircraft, we noticed right away that there were no passenger seats, as you would find aboard a commercial flight. That water purification unit took up the entire aircraft. There were a few bench seats with seat belts, but on a nine- or ten-hour trip that was not going to do well for us. We had to be in those seats for takeoffs and landings. However, after we were in the air, we looked around for anything that might be a little better than those jump seats. We ended up on top of the huge crates carrying the cargo. At least we were able to recline, uncomfortable and dirty as it was. By the time we reached Honolulu we were absolutely filthy. We looked like we had just climbed out of a roll-off dumpster we had slept in all night.

Just the trip itself was pretty amazing. The aircraft was a C-97, referred to as the "pregnant guppy." It might be easier to visualize if I described it as a fat blimp with short wings. It's as short as it is fat. To look at it, you would never think that it could actually fly. After taxiing down the runway for fifteen or twenty minutes, it was ready for final takeoff. It lumbered down the runway, very gradually gaining speed. Honestly it took so long to get up to speed I thought we were going to drive to Hawaii. When we reached lift-off speed, it honestly did not feel like we were going fast enough to leave the ground, but sure enough it lifted slowly into the air. I'm still not sure how it stayed up, and, when you are flying out over the Pacific Ocean, you really would like it to stay aloft.

We had made room reservations at Fort DeRussy BOQ (bachelor officer quarters) right on Waikiki Beach! What more could one ask for? We had free transportation to Hawaii, it would cost us just a few bucks a day for accommodations, and we were there for at least three days of rest and relaxation, or whatever we felt like doing. Is there any nicer place to be than Waikiki Beach for that price? I think not! Although it rained most of the time we were there, we did not let that stop us from making the most of it.

We rented a Volkswagen Bug and drove all around the island, including the famous North Shore. We had a great time and most of it was compliments of the US Army and Air Force. Where but in the military can you get away with that kind of action and do it legally? All right, today you might not get away with all of that, but opportunities abound, and when they do arise, we in the military should feel obligated to seize the moment. In any case, is that wild? Is that crazy? You bet, and I loved every bit of it. The military life can be an action-packed adventure. Yes, there is the good, the bad and the ugly, but it is a blend that most would agree can be a good life. There is always a need to accept the bitter with the sweet, in any walk of life, civilian or military.

## CHAPTER 10 – AFTER ALL IS SAID AND DONE

After one has gone through the whole military experience, what can be said of it, whether you have gone the career route to retirement or just a three or four-year enlistment or perhaps somewhere in between? Most of you have heard the old Marine motto, "Once a Marine, always a Marine." I can assure you that the same motto could be modified to include every branch of service. After going through the array of experiences and meeting the people you will have encountered, you will never be the same person you were before all of that. Your attitudes about life in general will be different, your appearance will be different, and in fact your entire demeanor will have changed remarkably. This will not have been a part of your life that you will ever forget or dismiss, or to which you will not continue to refer time and time again throughout the remainder of your life. It will have been and will always be a phenomenal part of your life. It really is part of who you are. There are always exceptions to every rule, but never allow the few who claim that the military was all bad for them to convince you that you should not consider the great possibilities that could be waiting for you.

Again, not trying to speak for all, I am sure that many of my readers will have similar feelings. Even though the US Army "kicked me out" several years ago (it's called mandatory retirement), I have never been able to refer to myself as ex-Army. I am still Army, but retired Army. People often ask me what my rank was when I got out. I answer with, "I did not really 'get out', but I am a retired lieutenant colonel." Had I not gone for retirement, but rather just a few years of service, I would still refer to myself as an "old Army guy." There is much more military blood running through my veins than civilian blood, even though I have been officially civilian for nearly twenty years now. My feelings might have been even stronger had I been on active duty all of those years, rather than in the reserve components. I'm really not even sure of that. Many of you may well attest to the same thing. You've been there, done that, and there is no way that most of you will ever truthfully claim that you are no longer a part of that life.

With regard to that after life (post military) I must again refer to my own experience. I wear my Vietnam veteran's cap, my retired Army cap or just a US Army cap, with my CIB, Airborne wings and Purple Heart pins attached, nearly everywhere I go, and believe me when I say that it is not just for recognition for anything that I have done, because, although it does feel pretty good when people walk up to me and say, "Thank you for your service," it is by no means the reason I wear it. I am amazed at the variety of reactions I receive from it. If you have never worn such a hat or observed anyone else wearing one for a long period of time, you will have no idea what I mean. As I mentioned, I wear a variety of hats, each depicting a different aspect of my service. On one, you can see the one-inch, yellow, block letters of VIETNAM VETERAN from a half block away. I don't wear that one often, and yet I get more responses from it than any of the others that are a bit more subtle. Why, you may ask, is that important? Allow me to elaborate.

When people see me on the street, in a restaurant, on a job site, in church, or anywhere else you can think of, I receive a wide array of looks.

1.) The blank stare. This is the one that may take the most interpretation. It could be a young person who is not quite sure what a Vietnam vet really is. He may well be thinking, "That sure sounds familiar, but I'm just not quite sure what that was all about." He may also be thinking, "What kind of person is this? Most of those guys, everybody knows, came back either chronic drug users or neurotics who could go on a shooting rampage at the drop of a hat." That's pretty much what my wife thought when she found out a few weeks after we met that I was a Vietnam vet. The minds of these individuals may be moving much faster than we think; they may well be wondering what I did all the time I was in the war. They may well be thinking, "Was this guy some kind of Rambo who was involved in clandestine operations in Cambodia, or was he a tunnel rat, a door-gunner on a helicopter, a pilot, a tanker or a desk jockey?" Indeed, your imagination is the only limit to what these people might be thinking.

2.) The disgusted look. This one is not terribly difficult to interpret. It would probably belong to the old peace lover, the people we called "peaceniks," and/or anti-war activist, either past or present, possibly both. They hate anything that has to do with the war machine, and that probably includes anyone in uniform. Most of them have no respect for the leaders of our country, no respect for the country itself and more than likely no respect for themselves. They basically hate everything you stand for, so there is probably not much hope for them anyway. It may also be the person who dodged the draft or managed somehow to stay away from becoming involved in the military, and now regrets it and has negative feelings about anyone who fulfilled their obligations. On the street they are almost literally staring daggers at you. It's all they can do to walk past you without saying something ugly, and, I am truly sorry, but it is rather fun to watch. They are so terribly uncomfortable, and, if you can handle it, it can "warm the cockles of your heart" to watch them. That does sound a bit cruel, doesn't it? Yeah, well, moving right along...

3.) The intrigued, curious or perplexed look. This is the one that is accompanied by nothing but question marks all around his or her face. They cannot figure you out for the life of them, not that anyone could ever figure me out anyway. The point is that person is very fun to watch too. I try to imagine all the questions that must be running around in his or her mind. "Who is this guy? Why is he wearing that hat? Is he trying to tell the

207 — After All Is Said And Done

world that he is some kind of hero? Is he trying to tell the world not to forget that there was another war a few years back that we are trying our best to forget ever happened? I wonder what he did in that war. Is he even a Vietnam War vet or is he one of those who wears the hat and never saw that country, but would like others to believe he had?" Why does that person look so intrigued? Who knows, but it really is interesting and fun to try to figure it out.

4.) The wide-eyed, extremely interested look. This is usually a young person who starts out with, "You were in Vietnam?" I'll answer, "Yes, sir (or ma'am), I sure was." The very young will probably ask, "Did you kill anybody?" whereby I usually answer, "I don't really discuss that very much with many people; just about any other questions I'd be very happy to answer for you." Now and then I might answer with, "Only if I had to." Often that will be followed by, "What did you do over there?" Then we can have a real discussion. I can often share a few of the stories that are easy to share and are fun for the younger set, many of which are right here in this book. As many of us know quite well, for as many of the ugly things that happen in war, there are also many things about which we can laugh and joke, and many for which we can have very warm and wonderful feelings.

5.) The warm, friendly smile. This person, male or female, will walk right up to you and thank you for serving and helping to preserve our life style, and being in a hostile area when our country was in need, and taking all the grief that we did when we returned home from that war. Those are the people who provide veterans of any war with the real rewards of having gone through the experience.

6.) The half-smile, welcome home, brother look. This is the guy that walks right up to you, reaches out his hand, and says "Welcome home, brother." You know automatically that he too is a Vietnam veteran. He might well follow that by asking when you were there, with what unit, in what part of the country you operated and other related questions. You've made a new friend automatically. If you are smart, you will maintain contact with that person. I have not always done that, and I am sorry for it.

Why do I wear my Vietnam veteran or US Army hat wherever I go? I hope you can see why. It has become a part of who I am. It may seem to indicate who I was in the past, but the reality is that I am still that same person, just a little older. Sometimes responses are a bit disheartening, but more often than not they are heart-warming, and I do enjoy a few "warm fuzzies" now and then. It is a great way to reach out to some of your fellow comrades in arms, and, as I said earlier, to make a few new friends, very possibly in your own hometown. We all have people nearby with whom we have a great deal in common and don't even know it. There might well be other categories of people and reactions to my hat, but the bottom line is that I seldom receive no reaction whatsoever, and I like that.

There are so many intangibles that one takes away from military experiences that it is impractical to try to list them in a single book. One of the most important is just being able to share some of those experiences with other people, particularly young people. You might think that they would have little or no interest in that kind of thing, particularly considering how long ago the Vietnam War was, but that is by no means true. I recall very clearly when my interest in the military first came to the surface, and I was a very young man. I must have been nine or ten years old when I watched my cousin's boyfriend, later to be her husband, progress through college Air Force R.O.T.C., become a second lieutenant, go through flight school and fly B-52 bombers. That seemed to me to be the most exciting thing a person could ever do with his life, and that is exactly what I planned for my life from that point on. That goes into a whole different story, however.

With regard to sharing stories and experiences, those of you who are veterans will always run into other veterans who have had similar experiences to you own, and it is interesting and sometimes therapeutic to share some of those things and even to "compare notes." It's nice to listen to others and get further insight into those experiences and perhaps even take on a little different perspective of things as you see events from the eyes of others. It may be helpful to them, but also may well be helpful to you.

It seems always to be the people who keep to themselves and never share their negative experiences with others who have the worst problems, and lack solutions to them. Besides all that, of course, it is sometimes fun to share some of the lighter times among all those experiences to see how many others have some similar stories to tell. That is not to say that the heavier experiences should not be shared also, but with some people you do have to be much more careful with how much you share. For some it is extremely difficult to share those memories. Some will absolutely refuse to share any of their past. For those I feel badly. They are the ones who really need any help they can get, yet probably never will seek it after so many years have passed.

Honestly there are thousands upon thousands of people out there who are hurting badly as a result of their past war experiences, but in most cases it is probably not necessary. If only those people would be willing to share what's on their minds with others who have been through it, they would, more often than not, feel better about their past and be able to deal with it a great deal better than ever before. I've been doing it for years and have never had any major psychological problems, even though my wife might well argue that point (probably not, seriously). I cannot speak for all, because all of us are different, but it certainly has worked for me. Please believe me when I tell you that I have seen plenty of war with all the ugly things that go along with it. All of what I have written in this book is absolutely true. Many can handle it and many cannot. I have memories that will never disappear, but that is what they are. They will always be with me, and there is nothing I can do about it. It is reality and it is a very big part of who I am today. Why would I want to forget about it? I might as well resort to drugs if I am to take on the attitude of checking out from reality, and that is not my style. That is a weakness, and there is little or no excuse for it. If I offend anyone, then I apologize for that, but not for having a low tolerance for that sort of thing. Life is too short to waist. That too is who I am.

If you are a young person, still in the process of planning your life, and have not yet decided what you are going to do with it, let me at least advise you to consider the focus of this book, and do not eliminate at least the possibilities of the military as a starter. High school graduations come and go, and young people go through needless anxiety about what to do next. Perhaps college is not an option right after high school, or even an interest. Frequently the first job offer that comes along is the big decision for that point in time. The problem often, as I mentioned earlier in the book, is that that job seems to be pretty comfortable and that is exactly where that individual remains for entirely too long, perhaps for the rest of his or her life. There is, however, so much more to offer, but it takes initiative and maybe even a few risks.

Before I end this book, there is one more major benefit to completing military service that I have not yet broached, and again, it makes no difference whether you have completed a four-year enlistment or finished off a twenty- or thirty-year career, you will be entitled to educational benefits, which will be part of the Post 9/11 GI Bill. I am also one who took full advantage of the older GI Bill, and, after coming off of active duty and going into the reserve components, I not only took advantage of the pay I made with the US Army Reserve, as I became an instructor with a US Army Reserve School, teaching the NCO academy students, but I received checks each month I was in school at the University of Arizona to pay for my tuition and books. That was an invaluable source of income for me while I prepared myself for an occupation in secondary education, and I even went further with postgraduate studies until my educational benefits were depleted.

Those people who transition from the military today and are interested in furthering their education fall under the Post 9/11 GI Bill. The Post 9/11 GI Bill (chapter 33 benefits) is an education benefit program specifically for military members who served on active duty on or after September 11, 2001. Depending on an individual's situation, provisions of the program may include coverage of tuition and fees, a monthly housing allowance, a books and supplies stipend, Yellow Ribbon payments, college fund or "kicker," rural benefit payments and transferability to eligible immediate Family members (Spouse and Children). (This information was provided by My Army Benefits [The US Army official benefits website], as well as the educational benefits information that follows.)

Some of the newer GI Bill benefits did not exist before 9/11. The older bill did not include housing allowance, and you could not transfer your benefits to a spouse or children. How much in the way of entitlements is dependent upon how much active duty time was completed. It can also depend upon whether or not there were disabilities involved. With no disabilities, a person could have as little as 90 days active duty and still be entitled to limited educational benefits. With a four-year enlistment the entitlements would be at the maximum. The types of education are not limited to college. Approved training under the Post-9/11 GI Bill includes both undergraduate and graduate degrees, vocational/technical training, on-the-job training, flight training, correspondence training, licensing and national testing program, entrepreneurship training, and tutorial assistance. All training programs must be approved for GI Bill benefits. Basically, there are no limitations to where you can go with those benefits. With what you have acquired through your military experience, combined with furthering your education in any direction you desire, you have tremendous opportunities. There is a great deal more information available on line. One of the most informative sources is: www.gibill.va.gov/benefits/post_911_gibill/index.html

I have an additional recommendation for all of you, and I can certainly use myself as an example of what not to do in formulating your plan for life. Always set high occupational goals for yourself, but use caution when it comes to establishing that ultimate goal. I have already mentioned establishing at a young age my goal of becoming an Air Force pilot. My real problem was never establishing a contingency plan. I was young and stupid, and I again apologize if I offend any of you, but that is a fact of life. We are all stupid when very young. It goes with the territory; we just can't see that until later in life. We all say then, "Gee, if only I had known then what I know now…"

Well, don't be concerned about that; just go on with your plan and make a few of the mistakes that you are bound to make. We would not be human if we never made them. Indeed, that is how we develop into mature, healthy adults. However, always, always, always have a back-up (contingency) plan for if and/or when the big plan falls apart, because you just never know what can happen along the way; that is totally unpredictable. When my eyes went bad in high school, I had no idea where I was going from there. The Air Force at the time required 20-20 vision for flight school, and I felt that life had come to an end. I struggled for many years until the US Army opened my eyes to a whole new set of possibilities.

As you begin your plan for life, maintain those high occupational goals, and never let obstacles get into your path. If you do not like what you are doing, try something new. Throw your fears to the wind; not your caution, just your fears. If the new endeavor does not work for you, it is never too late to change. What do you suppose I am doing right now writing this book? If it works for me, I will take my writing to any level it will go. I am nearly seventy years old, retired and starting something totally new. If it is right for me, I'll go for it and take it to new heights; if not, then I will be off to other pastures, but not without a good fight for what I think is right for me. That is exactly what I recommend for you, and it has little or nothing to do with your age, sex or nationality. My brother-in-law retired from the US Coast Guard after thirty years, now over fifty years old, and he is starting college this semester under the GI Bill. You have aptitudes and abilities, many of which you probably have not discovered, and many of which you never will if you do not venture out and reach for those new avenues. Good luck with the rest of your life!

## About the Author

John McClarren is a retired US Army infantry officer, having served for over thirty years before his retirement as a lieutenant colonel. During his Army active duty career, after a year as an enlisted man, he was a training officer at Fort Polk Louisiana, an infantry platoon leader in the Republic of Vietnam, a plans and operations officer at Sixth Army Headquarters at the Presidio of San Francisco, and finally both a psychological operations officer and an infantry company commander with the Second Infantry Division in the Republic of Korea. After coming off of active duty he remained in the reserve components of the Army until his retirement.

Besides his military service, John graduated from the University of Arizona with a BA in secondary education, majoring in German and minoring in English. He did graduate work at the University of Arizona as well as the University of San Diego in the fields of German, secondary education and counselor education. He taught high school German and English at Torrey Pines High School, Del Mar, California for twenty years, where, as well as teaching, he was active in the local teachers' union as site representative for many years, as well as grievance representative for the teachers of the district. That ended his full-time teaching career, whereupon he moved his family to northern Michigan where he still lives today.

With the tremendous length and diversity of his military career, his educational background with a teaching career, and his phenomenal array of travels around most of the world, John McClarren could not be better suited for writing MILITARY LIFE: A SOLDIER'S PERSPECTIVE as well as his memoir, TAKING RISKS DEFINING LIFE, soon to be published. They are both naturals for him. He is an expert when it comes to military subjects and what the military is all about, and has included some excellent examples for nearly every subject he covers in his books. He is also working on a humor book and his first novel.

## Abreviations

AIT – advanced individual training

BCT – basic combat training

CIB – combat infantry badge

EIB – expert infantry badge

LIB – light infantry brigade

MOS – military occupational specialty

NCO – non-commissioned officer

NVA – North Vietnamese Army

OCS – officer candidate school

PF – popular forces

PTSD – post traumatic stress disorder

ROTC – reserve officers training corps

RPG – rocket propelled grenade

RTO – radio telephone operator

VC – Viet Cong

VMI – Virginia Military Institute

## THANK YOU

Throughout the development and preparation of this book there have been many people involved, not the least of whom is my wife, Debra, who has shown patience and encouragement through the rejections, the rewrites, and my requests of her to read portions of and the whole manuscript over several years. She gave me excellent advice for changes and a modification of the original introduction, and further help on evaluating the front and back covers.

My mother-in-law, Beverly Chase, was one of the first to read my earliest draft, and she provided some excellent comments and recommended changes, which I appreciated very much. She has given me encouragement throughout the entire process and it has contributed to the completion of the final project. She also did the artwork for my publishing company logo.

My youngest son, Scott, an Army veteran himself, read through the original introduction, and related to me that it was well written but didn't hook him immediately. He and his mother were in agreement and I was finally convinced that I had to put something up front that would grab my potential readers. They both suggested a firefight scene from a real battle in Vietnam. He also had very valuable input in regard to content about him and his acquaintances.

I want to thank Matt Sinclair, a freelance editor as well as an author, for his expertise, and editing. He did an excellent job, which also humbled me greatly. He provided superior guidance. He gave the book the genuine quality that the book deserved.

Charlee Vale provided the image and additional work that was used for the cover of the book. It was a great contribution, which developed into a very effective final product.

I met Philip Espinosa, an Army veteran, through the writers group of which I am a member. He ended up being the real source of information and expertise for self-publishing, both for electronic and print versions. He gave me much more information than I could even absorb at the time, being brand new to the publishing business. He volunteered so much of his time to provide me with everything I needed for success that there is no way I can thank him enough. He is an accomplished author in his own right.

Finally, I want to thank the members of my Birch Run, Michigan writers group. They are truly an inspiration for writing, and they have provided great feedback for many pieces that I have shared with them. I also thank them for enduring some of my more lengthy pieces at the meetings that always seem so short. They tolerate me like very few others would.

# DISCLAIMER

Limit of Liability and Disclaimer of Warranty: The publisher has used its best efforts in preparing this book, and the information provided herein is provided "as is." The publisher makes no representation or warranties with respect to the accuracy or completeness of the contents of this book and specifically disclaims any implied warranties of merchantability or fitness for any particular purpose and shall in no event be liable for any loss of profit or any other commercial damage, including, but not limited to special, incidental, consequential, or other damages.

Trademarks: To the extent this book identifies product names and services known to be trademarks, registered trademarks, or service marks of their respective holders, they are used throughout this book in an editorial or illustrative fashion only. In addition, terms suspected of being trademarks, registered trademarks, or service marks may also be used throughout this book. Use of a term in this book should not be regarded as affecting the validity of any trademark, registered trademark, or service mark, nor an endorsement of any product or service. The publisher is not associated with any product or vendor mentioned in this book.

Please note that much of this publication is based on personal experience and anecdotal evidence. Although the author and publisher have made every reasonable attempt to achieve complete accuracy of the content in this book, they assume no responsibility for errors or omissions. Also, you should use this information as you see fit, are advised to customize the information and recommendations to your own personal and professional needs and at your own risk. Your particular situation may not be exactly similar to the examples illustrated here; in fact, it is likely that they will not be the same, and you should adjust your use of the information and recommendations accordingly.